T0104656

Unrequited Love

The first poem in this book is a three dimensional poem. It is one poem with two other poems contained therein. The inspiration for having the privilege to be the writer of such a poem could come only from the author who so connectively weaved together the lines of such. The author of which is Jehovah God. This poem is a prayer I prayed one day through Jesus Christ that he would ask my father Jehovah for me. Scriptures were shared with me just before I prayed for such a thing as love. These scriptures were about Gods holy name (Psalms 83:18), the one in whom I should pray too, as well as to pray all things through Jesus Christ because he is our mediator between us and God. I was also shared the scripture from John 14:13,14; "Also, whatever it is that you ask in my name, I will do this, in order that the father may be glorified in connection with the Son. If you ask anything in my name, I will do it." This particular scripture made me believe that I could ask God for the right man for me. In my heart I secretly prayed that God would use me as well, for his purpose, and I had faith that he would answer me.

When I found that this poem contained another poem that quoted my fears about such a thing as love and then it also contained an answer to that prayer for love; I was scared to death and I tried to hide in the back of the garage behind some cases of product that were to be sold at the gas station where I worked, and was working when I found the time to write my prayer out in a poem to God. I was terrible with grammatical punctuation and felt that the comma was needed everywhere. I guess just so you could pause and reflect on what I was saying. I got bored at the gas station because the computers were down and I could not serve gas to anyone, so I decided I would separate each line at the comma point into two different colors just to make my prayer poem pretty to Jehovah.

It was when I was done and I got to looking that it really was too many commas so I was looking to take some out. Just for fun I would read the words that were in their own color. And there it was . . . God had written me back . . . me . . . why me was all I could ask now. I was scared of it and scared of God and I spent the next fifteen years denying that it was Jehovah who had answered my prayer, I said it was Jesus. But it was not Jesus. It was Jehovah. Every once in a while I would build up the courage to tell someone about the prayer truthfully as it was written and say Jehovah's' name, but most of the time I lied and said I prayed it to Jesus.

Well I'm not holding back now. I don't know what to expect out of people except the worst now in life, so, if that's what happens I can't say I'm not used to it. It has been fifteen years now that I am one of Jehovah's Witnesses and I am proud to declare his name in all the earth. I don't know what to expect since I know it is a unique writing. It is the only 3-dimensional writing I have ever heard of. And then my son goes and draws his impression of his mother after all these years that would turn out to be 3-dimensional as well. It is similar to the portrait he drew of me when he was three years old but now it captures my pain and sorrow of un-re-quited love. They say a picture is worth a thousand words; I guess I have a thousand words and a picture. In this book I could not afford the color red to show you this poem in color so I had to use **Arial Black** and *Calligraphy*. My artwork within this book should have the color red in them as well just like the cover. In order to understand the 3-dimensional poem you first read the prayer poem as it is written and then you read the words in **Arial Black** only, these were my fears of what I prayed for. After that you read the words in *calligraphy* only, this is the answer to my prayer.

Lisa

THE PRAYER

Jehovah
Somewhere *in my world,*
Is this man *in my dreams.*
His eyes *are of understanding,*
His smile *of appreciation,*
Hands *so gentle,*
And body *so sweet.*
Trust **in me.**
Faith **in me.**
Love **for me.**
This man **in my dreams,**
Will he stay *in my dreams?*

In Jesus name I pray, amen.

Just the words in Black Arial:

Somewhere
Is this man
His eyes
His smile
Hands
And body
In me
In me
For me
In my dreams
Will he stay

Just the words in *calligraphy:*

4

In my world
In my dreams
Are of understanding
Of appreciation
So gentle
So sweet
Trust
Faith
Love
This man
In my dreams

Lisa
1985

THE CHANGING

My heart must withstand a wound for my soul to bare,
Only alone.
Slowly made deeper to cloud my judgment of the good I've
been
Shown.
Each experience stabbed sharper than the latter,
Emotions and morals bled and scatter.

A silver dagger with a silver blade.
Within the strength of a gentleman's hand,
A dagger of pain lay.

Intuition screams RUN!
I know this man and know what he holds.
A fear in me that burns as the fire in the sun.

Blinded with charms, a scornful mask.
Offering all—that I'd so easily ask.

I feel, but I cannot see.
I feel . . . him, needing me.

Love for this man found in soul, body and mind.
Now I stand silently, feeling only a need,
To hide from the dagger that has made me bleed.

Lisa
January 19, 1987

THE DEATH OF SOUL

To him she went as a soul.
She had left the body and mind to save the heart from loneliness.
"Oh Lord, why can I not run after my precious soul, to save her, her
Death of innocence?"
"Where is she . . . my soul"?
"Lord does he hold her"?
"Does he love her"?

To this you have listened each day my Lord.
In you I'm in love, you are adored.
For you love the lonely heart,
Who put to death my precious soul,
Who now lay in love
Of what she shall forever know . . .
That you are the coffin,
I've buried my soul.

Lisa
1987

Lisa

The Storm

Lonely rode in on a horse pale gray,
Her eyes sad black and very far away,
Maiden of Misery I had called her by name.
And asked of the lady what reason she came?
No word had she spoken,
Nor sound had she made.
Her tears were her tokens of time that had fade.
Her arms had held me in a cold embrace.
Her tears were warm as they touched my face,
And she would whisper . . . silently . . .
That I am her . . . and she is me . . .

THE LADY

Lisa
April 25, 1989

TIMES BRIDE

She reached for Time,
He'd touch her hand,
Has strength his own,
He helps her to stand.
Tells her he loves her,
Likes her his own.
Maiden wedded him sir,
Now she is Times alone.
The storm of her eyes gently rains,
As bride in his hours,
Each second ordained.
Who has found what is hidden and kept?
Who knows where love had fell?
Though tears of heaven are gently wept,
The bride hides forever in veil,
Never to fail in keeping time with her Lord.

Lisa
1991

IN A MOMENT OF THOUGHT

Look over my love,
You have no need.
I am there but I am not,
Can you find me?
From you I have hidden.
Where is my mirror?
Mirror of me?
My eyes have burning.
It burns!
Hold my hand.
My eyes are burning.
Where are you?
I love you.
I don't know.
I don't know.
Why did I always stay by him?
I don't know.
He was there.
Where are you?
I can't see,
I don't know,
I don't know where you are.
Morning hurts my eyes!
Blind sun!
NO I won't!
I'm telling the truth.
I feel.
Where am I now?
Are you there?
Talk with me.
Who is with you?
What do you need?
My eyes?
When will you need me?
Never need me?
When will you leave me?

Lisa

Come summer?
Fine . . .
Then my mind may sleep.
Rest . . .
Cool rest.
Wind blowing.
Breeze . . .
I am a soul.
An only soul . . .
Where are you?

Lisa 1989

THE VEIL OF SECRECY

Night full of dreams,
The looking glass is what it seems,
And the words, they are of marble stone,
Yet the man through the looking glass is not alone.
In the night he sings to me withdrawing the veil of life and death.
Taking not one more breath.
The first and the last,
From the deepest depth.
A dream memory.
A veil of secrecy.
I realize through the looking glass,
Deeply starring into me,
Present, future and past.
Just one breath it would be.
Oh veil of tears that do cover . . .
Life's joy and death's mystery;
Now come has my lover,
My peace and joy to be free.

Lisa
1990

WHOEVER'S LISTENING

Walking straight through this unlived life,
All the way to things beyond,
Always wondering when— where have you gone.
Searching for something I don't know what is,
Loving friends and trying to look above . . .
Love.
Got to see if everything they say is true.
But if in even who knew . . .
Why no one would understand.
Cause,
None of it was.
But I believe it will cost seventy-five cents.
Just a box of chocolate mints
For on the way,
Just for one day.
Gone.
In tomorrow,
Including all the things of sorrow.
Why?
Even bother to smell the flowers on the way,
And write a sentence the wrong way?
Why not?
The F I got in college or a pill I took for knowledge.
Was it, there it was.
Confession.
Of the death of beauty do children know of.
Tomorrow's flowers from the rain of love.
The imperfection and our own sorrow,
But the children still dance for tomorrow;
And no one knew what I was speaking of.
Well I am sorry, but it's hard to speak of love.
Quote,
On nothing that you think you know,
Or forget where you go.
Yesterday . . .
Brought with you something that shined,

Even to the blind.
So walk on,
Walk on . . .
You got beautiful things to see.
Lover, friend, whoever's listening . . .
Take me. I want to go.
Living . . .
Yesterday . . . Today . . . and Tomorrow.

Lisa
1991

Isa and Im

WHISPERS

Did you hear me tell you what I feel,
    Tell you of a need,
    Let you know I needed held,
    Afraid to show you that I bleed?
Did you hear me kiss you when you came near,
    Touch your hand,
    Love beyond the fear,
    Tenderly love a gentle man?
Did you hear me trembling from the way I feel,
    Cry softly of love and pain,
    Ask for a love that is real,
    Whisper again and again . . .

Lisa
1992

NO ONE

I have got no one here by my side.
No place in where I might hide.
No one to dry my tears,
Nobody to keep me from my worldly fears,

No one quite like you,
No one that is true.
No one to hold my hand,
No one to help me stand.

I have got no place to call my own.
I've got no place to call home.
I have no family there for me,
I have nothing but bad memories.

Nothing quite like you,
Nothing that is true.
No one by my side,
No place I could hide.

I have something special in me,
So deep not just anyone could see.
I have love deep in my soul,
I'm here for you if you need a place to go.
I'll be here by your side,
I'll give you a place to hide.
I'll make you a sweet memory,
I've got more love than anyone has ever seen.
No one, no one,
There isn't anyone quite like me.

Lisa
1994

THE HOMELESS RYTHEM

Crazy places and lost in time,
Strange faces and their crossing lines,
Weird visions take the forward road,
Hard rhythms of the homeless soul.
Hold me, hold my hand.
Pray for me in my broken stand.
The hearts wild the child will grow.
May we sleep in a place we know.
Five pointed stars paint the night.
Wishful things of gold moonlight.
Midnight canvas of sleep serene.
Milky way covers, my child dreams.
Help me wipe away the tears,
Rainfall dreams and sleepless fears.

Lisa
1994

LOVES' END

For strength and power
Deceive the hour
Of her sadness.
Her life and love
Are not her leaning towers
But a rode to madness.
She has grown use to her strange lover,
She pretends he's there . . .
Beneath the pillow and the cover.
She can't find the words she wants to say.
When it's just pretend
It's the lonely game you play.
Someday he will hear her,
She wonders when?
For in his love her tomorrow's yesterday,
Her today will never begin.
Today . . . loves end.

Lisa
July 1993

THE DEATH THRONE

Day after day of used measure
Time takes his pleasure seeing me alone.
My life locked in Times treasure
Buried beneath the death throne.

Somewhere in the darkness my soul has turned away,
Deep within the emptiness he calls me out to play,
He sings a gentle song as he ties' me by the hands,
Of how much he loves me, immeasurable as the sands.

He kisses me sweetly across my soul,
He whispers his secrets of where we shall go,
He puts on my finger a diamond stone,
And he builds my house beneath the death throne.

Lisa
November 27, 1995

GYPSY LIVING

Gypsy living,
Dying and giving
All of my dreams away.
Silently dancing,
Hopelessly romancing,
Listen to what I have to say.
Dying and crying,
I'm almost through trying,
I've got to go my gypsy way.
It's a hard way to live,
When your heart wants to give,
It's a hard way to die
Living the gypsy life.
If you think you've got to have it,
Then you'll get it for free.
If you are thinking about a habit,
You'll live it in the streets,
With fireflies in the skies,
Your dreams clouded up in your eyes,
Gypsy life's no surprise.
You are bleeding, your pleading, those gypsy lies.
Gypsy living
The Gypsy cries.

Lisa
1996

Lisa

Ina Ilene

THEIVING THE HEART AND CHALLENGING THE SOUL

Now I wouldn't be real would I?
Hanging on to my security,
Would it be my lie?
Remember my purity,
Bleeding as sure as I cry.
Everybody needs to break my soul.
Everybody wonders about what they don't know.
As I watch the video
Hope still lingers on.
Closing my eyes,
Refusing the hurt I've known.
Do you even try to touch me?
Or do you just think of how you can hurt me?
Maybe I'm missing the reason that you are smiling?
Guess I just don't do what you do.
You don't do what I knew.
In the name of the father,
In the name of the son,
Sparkling and fading,
It's got to be done,
With no boots on and black underwear.
As a fact, ask me if I dare?
I'm willing to break out a fifty
And bet my life you can't guess me.
In disguise,
In disposed,
As no one knows,
Leaving talents to find,
And leaving you behind,
To my face what would you call me?
One, two, three . . .
There is time to turn your eyes away,
As beauty croons to a clown,
There is no time to kiss and tell,
As the queen has fallen down,

Lisa

Does it have to be this way?
Some people just get torn apart,
Death is definitely around,
Still no one hears the sound
Of what I am trying to say,
Guess I'll just take it,
Guess it's my day.
I still have so much time to kill.
Life is so bitter, so very real.
Living in all my might,
I'm just looking to do what's right,
And yet here you are thieving my heart and challenging my
soul.

Lisa 1996

HADES BRAVE

Who shall soar down
And pick the earth from the ground?
Though the grave they find cold,
Not is the child within who is old.
He lay there weeping without ever being heard.
Screaming out but too soft to have word,
Alive with glowing eyes beneath the grave,
With clenched jagged teeth screaming,
A man lay long asleep dreaming,
Bound and chained as death thieves his breath . . . Hades
Brave.
The white silence of snow conceals his tomb,
His life is in living the skull king shadows of the morbid
womb.

Who shall soar down
And pick the earth from the ground?
Though the grave they have found cold,
Not is the child within who is old.
She lay there weeping without ever being heard.
Screaming out but too soft to have word,
Alive with glowing eyes beneath the grave,
With clenched jagged teeth screaming,
A woman lay long asleep dreaming,
Bound and chained as death thieves her breath . . . Hades
Brave.
The white silence of snow conceals her tomb,
Her life is in living the skull king shadows of the morbid
womb.

Who shall soar down,
And pick the earth from the ground?
Though the grave they have found cold,
Not are the children who are old.
They lay there weeping without ever being heard.
Screaming out but too soft to have word,

Lisa

Their eyes hold a mystery,
As love escapes death,
Before and after life history,
Still measure their breath.

Lisa
1994

So they let go and let God.
Silent and still for the words,
That breaks the madness of the shattering soul . . .
Was then that the smoke and veil
That hid the truth invisible,
And found naked . . .
Beautifully honest . . .
Yet unmovable . . .
Endless love of Jehovah God.

Lisa
1996

STANGE CADAVER

Hey You_____crossing alongside the road
Crossing the bridge
Who lost a life at a washed away ridge
Hey You_____down under the river dying again
You_____strange cadaver
You_____a believer
You_____a survivor
Hey You_____dragging you're stone
Your coffins your own
Hey You_____made of bone
Hey You_____does Misery know
Or has she lost her head
She can't take your soul
You're already dead
Hey You_____of yesterday
Hey You_____not alive or afraid of tomorrow
If you could just tell the living
The dead know of no sorrow

    Written for the victims of the flood of 93' of how the coffins of their dead were washed away.

Lisa
1993

JUNKYARD SAM

Junkyard Sam,
Build a dam,
And keep that river out.
Junkyard man,
Make a stand,
Show us—what it's about.

Desperate man with no gun or bullet around,
The garbage land and you with your hope down,
Your burning garbage can along the riverside,
Filled with sand and now your flames died.
Beggar man where can you be found?
Junkyard Sam,
Tell me you swam,
Or poor man, have you drowned?

Junk Sam should build a dam or cross that river.
Junkyard man to keep your land would be fish liver.
Poor man Sam light your logs,
Keep those wolves out,
Man, call your dogs,
Let Judas fight it out.
Desperate man with no gun or bullet around,
The garbage land and you with your head down,
Found no hand,
You lost again,
Poor man living in doubt,
Don't be a fool,
Don't be a king,
Find your way out.
Junkyard Sam,
Build a dam,
Keep that river out.
Make a stand,
Show us what it's about.

Lisa

This poem was written for those who worked hard fighting the flood of 1993 and for Junkyard Sam who might never have been missed for trying to save his cardboard home. I know you lived there old man river and with what very little money you did have you'd buy my junk things so my kid could eat. This is my only way to thank you and tell your family, whoever they might be . . . Sam is gone but not forgotten.

Lisa
1993

LONELY PLACES

Lonely places,
Lonely faces,
Sadness traces the depth of my soul.
Winning life's race, yes,
But I can't take this . . .
I really and dearly love you so.
Madness breaks us and we erase what might show,
If love embraced us where will it take us?
I too am afraid to go.

Lisa
October 1996

RELEASED

If I could make those clouds just disappear.
If I could get us way out of here.
Then maybe I could say that it won't rain,
Maybe that will take away our pain.
We could take a walk without any fear.
We could share the good times to brighten up the year,
Yet when I look straight in your eyes
My heart shatters, breaks and cries
With how you stand by me,
How it is you never deny me,
And then you go and say 'no sad songs here please'.
When on our knees you whisper 'hush now, no crying',
Too sing you glad songs, put your heart at ease, because no one's
Dying.
And when we sang those silent thoughts we heard whispered
Through the trees
I saw you smile at me and . . . and then you were gone just
like a Breeze.
It was then I knew that love is never kept . . . only released.

Lisa
1999

TAKEN IT

I've taken you in,
Don't ever let go.
It's a hard one baby,
It's a good thing baby,
Love is all we know.
You've give your love to me,
All the love you show,
I love you again,
I'm taken you in,
Don't ever let go.
I took it all in,
I'll never let it out,
I love you baby,
There could be no doubt,
I take you all in,
It's what loving is about,
Because you're my man,
Who'll never do without.
I love to love you in the morning.
I love you all through the night.
I've just got to let you in baby,
I'm not even going to fight.
I took it all in.
All the way I cried,
You know sweet baby,
You're hurting me inside.

Lisa
1996

Lisa

INDECISION'S DECISION

Somebody take me out of this nightmare.
I'm not going anywhere.
You save me from the cold grave,
If I'll stop screaming and behave.
I don't think I like what I envision,
Indecision's decision.
If I hadn't made a choice,
It would still be the same,
Just another nightmare,
Some other total head game.

Lisa
1988

Lisa

Ike

NEVER ENDING TORMENT

Time moves on in its' own way.
It sure is kind of funny the crazy kind of days.
As time passes by,
I kind of like to try,
A little piece of mind.
If I got the time.
It sure is strange trying to find the moment,
So much has got to change,
Never ending torment.

Lisa
1989

Isaiah

INDECISION'S DECISION
NEVER ENDING TORMENT

Somebody take me out of this nightmare.
I'm not going anywhere.
You save me from the grave,
If I'll stop screaming and behave.
I don't think I like what I envision,
Indecision's decision.
If I hadn't made a choice,
It would still be the same,
Just another nightmare,
Some other total head game.
Time moves on in its' own way.
It sure is kind of funny the crazy kind of days.
As time passes by,
I kind of like to try,
A little piece of mind.
If I got the time.
It sure is kind of strange trying to find the moment,
So much has got to change,
Never ending torment.

Lisa
1990

UP A HOGS BUTT FOR A HAM SANDWICH

"Dirty foul mouth welfare dysfunctional credent.
Life is a precedent diploma not an antecedent dogma.
The frustration, the fluctuation of life within,
Some must earlier begin.
Lazy drugged out somatic, schismatic, schemer,
There are those, whose lives are greener,
There are those who struggle to keep their demeanor,
Some never even find the door and, others just keep wanting
more . . .
                    Ham sandwich?
So strength to strong bound and keep your life turning
around.
You poor darn, low down, detrimental, demented, food stamp
fed, dirt head flunkies;
Prison bound, fatherless found, pro life, no life, bar crowned
junkies.
Keep your head up on your road to freedom.
Needing help, dying, bleeding, pleading, somewhere
believing,
Keep your head up a hogs' butt for a ham sandwich;"
Said the volunteer at the soup line.
The homeless man politely refused the gentleman's noble
charity,
As he stated the following remark;
"With the greatest respect for myself, sir, as not to grovel for
my meal today,
As I see you are serving stone soup with your ham
sandwiches."

Lisa
1995

Lisa

Isaac

THE CRACKERJACK ANATOMY

In the crackerjack anatomy of the mind,
With friends who are dead or left behind,
I watch myself a fat bag of bones,
But, then looking at you I see that's all you own.

With skin and hair and brain and teeth,
With mind and spirit and heart beneath,
Gifts given and then taken away-
Oh! With bone and flesh let us play.
We jump and run and laugh and kill.
We kiss and hug and take our pill,
3x per day the doctor's way; with food or milk.
It may keep you alive but won't keep you in fur and silk.

It shall take the money and a lot you know,
But please try and hide it so the greed won't show . . .
How you made, why you made, when you made it-
Where you laid it.

The conscience is watching and it will tell . . .
It will weigh it out and start to yell!!!
Only for you and your life;
They've got their own . . . your children and wife.

I'm not your judge nor can I see.
Everything you do you just want to be free.
Yet I, the conscience will never let that be.
I live within your bone and flesh.
I walk with you to talk you out of life's' strange mesh.
I hope will walk the perfect line,
But in the end we're both a dying.

Lisa

In the crackerjack anatomy of the mind,
With friends who are dead or left behind,
I watch myself a fat bag of bones,
Yet to look at you I see that's all you own.

Lisa
1999

INTO THE WIND

Should someone give meaning to all that I've learned,
Each day that I cry should I have to return?
Someone to worthy the struggle that lives so vain,
Then there I should realize I have been called by my name.

Could something bring back the joy there was to learn,
Or the thought that I suffer was wisdom I earn.
To cry and release the pain from the sorrow,
To wake up and thrill to live a new tomorrow.

In silence I reach for the words to put still . . .
The numb fear of breath that I draw in vain.
In madness I weep for the love that I feel,
As I know . . . know nothing human . . . to hold my hand.
Yes still we have called them a friend.
Yes, still we have called love to the end.

And I turn around and I turn around into the wind,
And I scream and I scream for my being to end.
And I turn around and turn around reaching out
for someone in the wind,
And I scream and I scream for my being to end.

Yet sadly I have awoken on a joyful new day.
Ungrateful for the emptiness I still live and pray.
I should be more thankful to breath it all in.
If I would be then will it end?
No, there is where it all begins.
For love of love to the loving end.
From love I came to love again.

And I turn around and I turn around into the wind,
And I scream and I scream for my being to end.

Lisa

And I turn around and I turn around reaching
out for someone in the wind,
And I scream and I scream for my being to end.

Lisa
2003

THROWING STONES

We cast our stones upon the water.
We watched them sink down so heavily.
At least one or two stones farther;
One for you and one for me.

They are there to sink beneath the blue,
The dreams we have thrown away.
Into the river of tears it is true,
My heart is a stone to stay.

To throw the first stone, you or I,
Across the rippling waters of life;
Now love has gone flying by,
God give you peace and your new wife.

Like a stone I stay here still
Beneath the river flow,
Someday something I may feel,
But just a stone I'll never know.

Lisa
2002

THE CHANCE

Dancing and romancing,
Different times I fell in love with chance
And I flew away.
Dreaming,
Disbelieving, we'd ever end up going our separate ways.
Love and look above my friend . . . its' another day.
When you are trying,
Just surviving,
There is no denying what is left to say.
When it is romance you dance with,
You take a chance that love would stay.

Lisa
1996

DEEP DOWN BABY

Deep down baby,
Down deep in my heart,
You would hide baby from falling apart.
Deep down baby,
Deep within me,
Your love cries out to this lady.
Why did you leave me?

Deep inside I've fallen apart.
Every space was broken when you filled my heart.
Down deep baby it had to be,
How hard we tried,
To keep one heart together when we both cried.

Deep down baby,
Down the road,
Feeling our love eternities old,
You'll always have that part of me,
That let you die and set you free.

He said way down baby . . .
Deep down . . .
Lay down baby,
Let me inside.
Deep down baby,
Deep in you,
I'm loving you lady . . .
Do what you got to do.
Deep down,
Way down,
Deep inside,
I've laid down my life . . .
For you I have died.

Lisa 1998

Lisa

THE TRUTH HURTS

I try to break it down . . .
What it is you have done to me.
I try to shake it somehow . . .
But through these tears I just can't see.
I run to Jehovah,
To tell him how I feel.
I say, "Oh Lord please tell me this is a dream,
That it really isn't real.
I have gotten so weary,
So deep in my mind,
My soul so heavy to carry,
On this torture stake I'm dying."
I can still hear him saying . . .
"Lisa . . . I love you."
Now I am hanging here praying,
"Jehovah, in the name of Jesus Christ . . .
Is this not really true?
Through the name of Jesus Christ, my father Jehovah,
Is this not really true?'

Lisa
1998

MEASURE LOVE

Night moves . . . straight through you and I.
Though the sun has descended,
Hearts have been mended,
We won't ever say goodbye.
Its' breeze blows over our mind
As we unwind to a song.
Its' rhythm is beautiful and kind,
Its' measure long.
How sweet the night air,
So bright is the star sitting there.
Birds of a breath,
You're taking flight,
And you are my song,
No baby, there is nothing wrong.
The breeze you are flying on
Has us all singing along.
The flight that we take
It is the song we make
Upon the night air.
Soaring through these wind full melody songs,
Lets me know there is nothing wrong.
Sing to me till the sun comes along.
Fly me upon the winds of your throne,
Save me my baby from being alone.
Oh baby sweet baby sing me your songs . . .
The musical rhythm of the measure of love.

Lisa
1994

MAN IN THE MOON

Do your dark lonely dances around the moon,
Your sadness romanced you,
Swept you away too soon.
In love with the madness that holds you insane,
Now you can't even remember his name.
Who is this?
Who is this man in the moon?
Why doesn't he marry you in June?
Who is this?
Who is this man in the moon?
Is he coming around here soon?
Will he take you for a ride in his limo around the moon?
You should try and find his love very soon.
The moon rises and falls,
But you don't know why,
Or why the kiss of your breath goes to the guy in the sky.
Who is this?
Who is this man in the moon?
Why doesn't he marry you in June?
Who is this?
Who is this man in the moon?
Will he be coming back around here soon?

Lisa
1993

Imre Idan

THE SPARROW

I saw a sparrow beaten by the storm.
She was bloody where her wing had been torn.
Somehow someone grabbed the knife,
Cut the sparrow from her bloody life.
I saw . . .
A man pick her up and squeeze the dead bird in his hand,
As if there were still life for the bloody man.
A song came from the bird,
Singing one word . . . alive!
The man ripped open the sparrow to stop the song,
Alive is the sparrow that was dead all along.

Hey mister, why don't you put that bloody sparrow down?
You know mister she can't fly around.
What kind of life is this that you have found?
How do you hold to something that dies?
Alive with respect—let it fly.

Lisa
1993

Lisa

FULL CIRCLE

Such a twisted licorice stick,
What a tormented wasted trick.
The tongue stay stuck to this chewy chocolate mint.
The life goes switching from heaven to hell bent.

The arm seems perplexing to the hand.
The leg to the foot says, "you're going to have to make your
stand."
The knees to the floor cry in pain.
The mind to the heart says, "life in vain."

The heart to the truth dreams of lies.
The soul to the angels tell goodbye.
The hope left crawling on the floor,
The humble left to find the door.

Some wise to wonder turn around.
Some gifted still thunder above the ground.
Some seek demented reality.
Still others know that grace shall be.

Don't fail to see the turn of tides.
Cross the full circle in wisdoms' stride.

Lisa
1990

THE GAME

I knew these games way back when,
When I met others just like you in sin.
And still, they lost them all to me
Because I play no games,
That's the way you win, just to be.

Still, I kept you all as friends,
Because enemies should be in my front or side,
Or they'll have my back in the end.
Although I really wanted something true . . .
I tested and tried but found it not in you.
It was what I suffered that showed me why,
A friend can be just a friend until the games gone by.

And now you know the game is done.
And I just couldn't be beat.
Very few true friends had been won.
But my enemies lost in the meet.

Lisa
2004

Lisa

THE SEASON

Come the falling of the leaves,
Shine of the moon,
Fall wind air,
Whispering death to its' tune.
It is the season . . .
I turn like the leaves,
Only to see one who grieves.

He's softly whispering my name to the wind.
His love of me he wishes to send.
Blackness of night,
Dark as coal,
Alone he is standing,
Within barren trees,
Needing,
Needing . . .
The feeling,
Healing,
Of my soul,
He silently screams his hurting plea.

My love,
I see you alone and cold.
When the season has stole away our love you have come to
know,
Feeling the fall air,
Reach to your heart and feel me there.

It is my season, the season is me.
I am the barren trees',
The shades of the leaves,
The sudden wind air,

The watchful eye of the moon,
I am there . . . with you.

I love you.

Lisa
1986

Lisa

HONESTY AND GRACE

Haughtily he laughed into an honest face.
His pitiful attempt to reflect her grace.
So to the mirror of his laughter,
She told him of his morrow,
How each day before and after,
Is his true reflection . . . sorrow.

Lisa
1989

IF TEARS HAD A SOUND . . .

I would know the pain, the heartache, and the suffering deep within your soul that I will have brought to you I know. I will bring my heart and soul close to your spirit, so as to take away these things I have brought to you from carelessness, disrespect, and, with no gratitude for the times that you would stand with me, before me and, beside me.

Lisa
1987

Lisa

TIMES OF WINE

Sitting peacefully with friends of mine,
Sipping warmth from a bottle of wine.

Friends of care could you figure my mind,
Why will I drink wine of this kind?

Each of you I gave a glass,
And filled it with memories of times in the past.

Each of us are family to the other . . .
As I am your sister . . .
You are my brother.

A toast to the few!
Time has seen my strength come from you.

If your glass should empty,
One will be there,
And fill it with a time of wine.

Savor the wine . . .
Its' vintage is of only a time.

How bittersweet this love in its' time,
How funny the taste,
How smooth and fine.

The crystal rings,
The goblet chimes.
The love sweet,
Times of wine!

The glass was raised,
The toast was said,
Stayed in our hearts . . .
All of our dreams ahead!

Lisa
1987 and 1997 and . . .

Lisa

BARREN AT SEA

There is a ship sailing lonely at sea.
Sailing for land if there may be.
The water is cold and miles deep.
The heights of the waves are so very steep.
The cold wind on our face,
"Please shelter us Dear Lord,
There is no ship captain,
Just a woman and child aboard."

Lisa
1989

SWEET SHADOW

Sweet shadow I never know where you are.
Never knowing how far you have to go to hide,
Before you find that someone is by your side.

Sweet shadow I never know where you are,
If you've gone too far from where you want to be.
You should be wanting to stay with me,
In your place next to me,
Still your acting like you can't be free.

My darling shadow how is it you'll ever find,
A body more sweet to you,
A soul more kind?
Keep holding onto me,
Sweet shadow,
Through all time, just let it be.

Every time I turn around,
My shadow is running away.
I try to lift you up off the ground,
But there you seem to want to stay.

Please hang on sweet shadow,
Just keep trying,
You'll find it is better than letting go,
Anything else is only dying.

Even with my back to the wind . . .
Shadow be true,
I'll see you again,
Even though it may seem I don't want you.

Lisa
July 8, 2004

SEPARATED . . . BY THE LOVE IN ME

Shadow . . . she was on the run,
But I shot her dead beneath the sun.
I watched her body shake in pain,
And now I am not the same.
She's never coming back,
And I keep losing track of how we tried to make it.
I never really understood if our love was good,
But I know I can't hate it.
Why did you leave me in so much pain laying there?
Didn't you want me lady?
Did you ever even care?
Or did you just want to drive me crazy?
No I never really understood if our love was ever good,
But I know I couldn't have hated it.
And yet still we separated.
I suppose you believe it was for the best,
Left to the test,
Cause I could no longer make it to the challenge that was so
deep inside.
So tender in you all I could ever do was cry.
So what am I going to do?
I keep trying to just live on through and hope that I can make it,
Before I again get separated . . . by the love in me.

Lisa
2003

SUICIED

So many . . . to not be a friend.
Of course you are . . . in the end.
So many . . . turning to the other,
Of course they care . . . one friend to another.
So many . . . who held out there hand,
Of course they took . . . what helped them to stand.
So many . . . who saw me cry,
Of course they would . . . walk by.
So many . . . looking in at me,
Of course they should . . . one to see.
So many . . . wondering why?
Of course today they do . . . but I don't cry.
So many . . . reaching out,
Of course to touch . . . my fears and doubt,
So many . . . to feel empty and cold,
Of course they signed . . . the register told.
So many . . . now hating my ever being,
Of course they think . . . that this I'm seeing.
So many . . . now understand,
Of course I am too . . . a cold hand.
So few . . . should bare for me a genuine sorrow,
Because I am the one deciding no tomorrow.
So few . . . should shed a precious tear,
Of course from the way I chose to leave you here.
So few . . . need not even try to understand,
Because I could take my life with my own hand,
So few . . . shouldn't even think to care.
It will just drain you . . . you'll still just be standing there.
So few . . . should ever really pray from their heart to the Lord
for me,
Because I am the one who must face what I have done you see.
None at all . . . should even cry . . . I am the one who chose to die.
It's too late for all that now.

Lisa 1988

FACE IT

An ear use to listen,
An ear now closed,
A mouth used for kissing,
Now only thinks it nose,
A nose never smelling,
What the mouth should be telling,
That the eyes never saw,
That love and only love could know at all.

Lisa
1988

LOVE THE RIDE

Spinning in my head,
Spinning instead,
Of falling on the ground,
Of crawling through this town,
Turning life around,
Living with what I found.
Faster than before,
Faster, living more.
Loving! Having fun!
Living on the run.
Running from this place,
Turning away my face.
Hope you'll be by my side.
Hope you'll love the ride.
Flying far from here,
Forgetting all the tears.
Turning loose the years,
Letting go of fears,
Jumping on the bike,
So you can take a hike,
Because it's more than just something I like,
I love the ride!

Lisa
1999

Lisa

LET IT RIDE

We're going my way,
The blockhead in a sleepy little southern town,
The nape of leather and a little beer;
The family members near,
We're all related at the rally.
It's all coming down.
The pills in the alley and defenders of the peaceful task;
The death is here and Katmandu wore a mask.
The heroes of the ground;
From the luring Tawangos to the jungles of Ran boon,
Pan Head you're the knucklehead of them all.
America said, "The war won't be small"
1942 The Harley rode through with the spirit of it all.
Hell Angel breaking the rules,
Motor riding with death tools.
Death . . . perceived by trillions.
Life . . . deceived by millions.
So where are you going?
I'm on the ride man.
On a Christmas run.
Going to make a stand!
Going to have a hell of a lot of fun!
So you own a Harley?
It's a ride on a comets tail,
Its' one part love—two parts trail.
Riding the Flathead,
With no help wanted and no food stamps,
Death is certain and life is your chance.
Road struggling with the flag,
A teardrop tank,
The image of the reaper,
The Chopper,
The drag,
The crank,
The smoke of the creeper,
The rebel "BMRC" around the world,

With the wind unfurled around him,
Riding for a love-in where Free Flocks Fly.
Cooperate America will never die.
The Harley gangs around,
We're riding . . .
Doing what must be done,
Learning how to survive,
Looking at the face of the future,
Staying Alive.
The bad ones riding alive with nothing to fear,
The Harley you hear . . .
The world belongs to all,
Surveillance is near and its' eye shall see,
You and I riding it free!
Jack, Brando and James Dean,
Love the ride!
Let it ride!
Let it be seen!

Lisa
1992 (A poetic chronicle of the history of the Harley Davidson)

Lisa

Id

CRUEL JOHN

He has no soul,
Shares no heart,
Out of control,
Except just to break you apart.
He lives inside you,
And will only move on,
Ever so silent,
Cause you're the one . . .
Who enjoyed him with love.
He'll touch you deep,
To tie himself to your soul,
While he goes free, you,
He will never let go.
Around his finger you have been twisted and tried.
Before his eyes you will have begged and cried.
Still no sound will he ever hear,
The feel of love is not what he will fear.
It's how he reaches out and loses control.
His loss of power,
His loss of soul,
As he leads a cruel dance of love and lies,
And pretends Cruel John feels nothing inside.
The dance never ends though the rhythm does change.
The heartbeat driven weak,
The feeling so strange,
Though the mind runs away you shall remain his young woman in hand.
The heart starts to pray not to give in,
Yet he sweeps you away with his softer side,
Bittersweet is the dance, you can't take it in stride.
Still you found so softly your soul in his hand,
And now Cruel John has so deceitfully made himself your man.
Slow dancing your heart to the rib from his side,
He whispers in your ear, "How cruel . . . my lady love has died."

Lisa
2004

ANGELS PLEAD OUR CASE

The world is a bitter place.
It takes more than its giving,
And no one is making a living here.
Everyone has got a gun,
They don't take anything from no one.
Children live in fear.
The world is a bitter place,
Another friend dies before our face.
Where is the strength to say goodbye?
Struggling through the need to cry,
Somehow we wipe away our tears,
And yet, nothing to forget the bitter years.
The world is a bitter place.
The dead score the livings' race.
The angels plead our case,
You can't replace those who once were here
But you can retrace the steps they had to take in fear.
The world is a bitter place,
The angels plead our case . . .
The end is near.

Lisa
1995

TAKE A CHANCE

Dancing and romancing,
Different times I fell in love with chance,
And I flew away.
Dreaming, disbelieving,
We'd ever go our separate ways.
Love and look above.
My friend, its' another day,
I hear your trying just surviving.
There's no denying what is left to say.
It's a chance for romance and you just play.
When its romance you dance with,
You take a chance that love would stay.
Dancing and romancing,
Different times we fell in love with chance,
And we flew away.
Dreaming we keep believing.
Love is that way.
There's no crying,
We're just trying to make love stay.

Lisa
2002-2004

Lisa

DEAR LITTLE PAPER CLOWN,

Why is only you that be around? I bet you could never guess just what is wrong inside? I've talked to you the most so you know it couldn't hide. Boy—he doesn't ask, so now I write it down . . . for the only one who listens, my little paper clown. I wish for me you'd paint a smile, for no one but you has held me in so long awhile. And you . . . the only one I touch; but no kiss could I steal from you little paper clown . . . you just can't feel. Looking into my eyes can you see that I've been hurting? The comic of my lies though I smile when I'm flirting? Can you understand me paper clown? Can you see my paper frown? It is you paper clown who loves me when I'm down. No one to me could listen but to me you listen good. It is me you be kissing, I'd smile if you would? Then a comic you'd be lies . . . your smile would be flirting . . . you'd smile with my eyes . . . together we'll be hurting.

Love 'I PAGLIACI'

(Was continued in 'I PAGLIACI')

Lisa
1985-2004

PAPER LOVE

There is a fascination with paper,
I just can't explain.
I have it written in poems and drawn in art.
I keep it deep within me as well as set it free.
I do my best to give it some sort of form,
It is the best form that I can believe.
Once it is written or drawn . . .
Perhaps even in the air as a song,
It is no longer a leaf.
It is my hope that it may become a part of many branches of a tree.
A shady tree,
A cool spot to rest,
Gods' blessing shading you and me . . .
Poet Tree.
With a twig I write it down,
I learn to stand up straight and keep good ground.
I give my life to what I have found.
The clouds are my horizon with Gods' grace as endless bounds.
For this I thank him for the words,
As birds they live in Poet Tree.
And I thank him for the unanswered prayers that kept me free.
AMEN.

Lisa
1993

Lisa

THE BRAND NEW DAY

If times weren't so tough,
Maybe we'd think life weren't so rough.
Every day we push on in the same old way.
We shower and look in the mirror.
We try not to think of the fear.
We have our coffee at the start of the day . . .
Cappuccino,
Express machine,
The news surprise . . .
Before our eyes.
So life tries at another sunrise.
No we won't think back
We try to relax
Take with you a new day.

But for now we will say, good night, good night.
Little girl sleep,
Tonight there are no more memories for you to keep.
Wake up bright a brand new day.
Don't look back upon dismay.
Good night, good night.
Little boy sleep,
Tonight there are no more memories for you to keep.
Wake up bright on a brand new day.
Don't look back upon dismay.

Tonight it is our love shall sleep,
And soundly within special memories so deep.
If Jehovah wills', the morning in our eyes will shine.
This is love through all time.
When we begin our brand new day,
It is then and there we each will say,
Good morning! Good morning love.

There is a day to come,
It seems long in waiting.
Anxious hearts, anticipating . . .
No pain inside,
No tears we cry,
The day of you and I.

Lisa
1986-2007

THE DAY OF THE REST OF MY LIFE
(Written by Nick Erickson) (My Son)

It is my mind, my world.
No one can ever destroy my world
Or your own . . .
                ERICKSON
Today is the day of the rest of my life,
Though it is but a small plight.
I will surely put up a tremendous fight,
For my future is in my sight . . .
                ERICKSON
As I see the dawn of my dream
I leave all the shame that my life,
This world,
This game has brought to my brain . . .
                ERICKSON
As I look around I fall to the ground . . .
                ERICKSON
Yet there is no sound for my pain . . .
Shall never bring me to the ground.
So when all is sorrow,
Look up and grab the hand of tomorrow . . .
                ERICKSON
The pain I feel,
The sorrow I see shall one day overcome me.
But that day will always be the day I am no longer me,
Because I know some will always love me . . .
                ERICKSON

February 20, 2002 1:27 p.m.

HARD TO HOLD

It takes a lot more to love me-yes it does.
It takes a lot more to love me-because of what I was.
I'm not the easy kind to play on your mind,
I'm not the virgin you were hoping to find.
It's a lot harder to love me-to give me what I need.
It takes a lot stronger man to heal the heart that bleeds.
(chorus)
And I----- I will stay in your soul.
And I----- I may hurt you so.

- - - - - - - - - - - - - - -.
I'm the kind of woman that wants what is real.
I'm the kind of woman that knows the deal.
I've done all the right things in all the wrong ways.
I haven't had an easy life and damn few easy days.
I have the kind of heart that always has hell to pay.
(chorus)
But I----- have just wanted love to stay.
And I----- for love have always prayed.

- - - - - - - - - - - - - - -.
And now the kind of woman they say that remains,
Is the kind of woman whose gone crazy for love and insane.
And now I----- can't find any man around.
And I ----- am left lonely in town.
And I ----- don' like what this seems,
I----- don't want what this may mean.
That I am the kind of woman left all alone,
A lot harder to love a lot harder to own,
So now if there was left anything for me,
I----- don't have a dream.
I----- feel nothing it seems.
(chorus)
I----- will stay in your soul.
I----- may hurt you so.

- - - - - - - - - - - - - - -.
I'm the kind of woman it takes a lot more to give.

I'm the kind of woman your afraid you won't know how to live.
I'm the one you are afraid to hold on to tight.
I'm the one that you say made you need your drugs at night.
I'm the one your afraid will get out of your sight.
I'm the kind of woman who might get away.
But I----- I'm really just a little girl at play.
And I----- I have only tried to love you that way.
And now it is I----- who will have hell to pay.
(3rd dimension background rhythm)
Your woman's been your child of the heart.
Just a woman but a child set apart.
Not your toy with a broken heart,
But now a girl torn all apart,
Little boy with no brave heart,
Who takes the doll and tears her apart.
Now he turns around and can't understand,
Why his woman won't hold his hand.
He's the kind of man too leave,
The kind of man . . . this kind of woman don't need.

Lisa
2002, 2007

ONCE HAD A DADDY

You left me standing in the rain.
You can't even see that I'm in pain.
I have nothing left to gain,
Because you left me standing in the rain.

I once had a daddy who understood.
He would give me loving you know was sooo gooood.
He'd give me what I need.
Love for nobody but me.
My baby, my daddy, so sweet.

With all these tears I have to cry,
There's no point in even asking why,
You're never coming back here again,
Or how you could leave your best friend.
You left me standing in the rain.

I once had a daddy who understood.
He would give me loving you know was sooo good.
He'd give me what I need.
Love for nobody but me.
My baby, my daddy, so sweet.

You left me standing in the rain.
God I hurt and feel so much pain.
This is hardly an easy thing,
Dealing with a broken heart
You left me drowning in the rain.

I once had a daddy who understood.
He would give me loving you know was sooo good.
He'd give me just what I need.
Love for nobody but me.

Lisa

My baby, my daddy, was sooo sweet.
I once had a daddy, he understood.
He'd give me loving you know was sooo good.
He'd give me just what I need.
Love for nobody but me.

Lisa
2005

BIG DADDY

Some people need big mansions.
Some people need big cars.
Some people need big tall drinks,
To drink up in big fancy bars.
But I just need my big daddy to understand one great big thing,
I don't need another big hole in my heart or them big ol' blues
to sing.

(CHORUS)
Big Daddy! In his great big blue caddy.
Big Daddy! Lord he's got to have me.
Big Daddy! In his great big blue caddy.
Big Daddy! Lord he's got to have me.

Some men love a big leg women to treat them right.
Some men love to take her to their great big house where she
can stay the night.
Some men love to flaunt their big bank account too,
But I just need my big daddy to understand one great big thing,
I don't need to sing the blues about the Great Big You.

(CHORUS)

So in or out of great big mansions,
Or in or out of great big cars,
With or without a great big drink
You got from your great big fancy bar.
Big daddy better have a great big thing for his girl with a great
big heart.
Or big daddy is going to get left in small pieces when my big
ol' blues' tear him apart.
Big daddy better have a beautiful song to sing
Because I'm a great big woman and I know how to swing.

Lisa
2005

GOD DON'T SING THE BLUES

Yeah, that's right, they got to dance,
And they got to sing.
They know how to act,
Yet nothing can change what God don't bring.

Everything is thought out,
And the explanation will fit right in,
And when the sun rises,
And your new day won't go by the rules,
So you got the blues, so you get to be the fool.

You know you're going to live it,
Just how ever you got to fit it.
You know they're going to have it,
However they've got to stab it.
And when tomorrows gone,
And everything has been said,
You'll still be the one who has to go on.

So you got to dance,
And you know you got to sing.
And you know just how to act,
With the words you're going to bring.
If it doesn't fit the world then the blues aren't what they sing,
But you know you feel it girl and you know you'll do your
thing.
If it makes you happy and others begin to smile,
Then dance, and sing, and act it girl, if only for awhile.

Cause you know we got to dance,
And you know we got to sing.
You know we got to act out the fool,

Cause the blues God don't sing.
No, the blues God don't bring.
No, the blues God don't sing.
The blues God don't sing.
The blues God don't sing.
No, the blues God don't sing.

Lisa
2006

Lisa

BUTTERFLY TEARS

Why baby when I reach out for you I just get turned away,
With many excuses and meaningless words you say.
There's no touching, nor talking, nor asking of you,
As if you have no heart that needed loved too.
I have not wished to become this painting on the wall.
Something to have around but just a pretty picture after all,
Why is it baby I cannot be more than just when you decide I'm
something you need?
Why should the rest of my life be lonely to lead?
I try to treat you fair when giving you the love that I have,
But the more empty I become the less you'll find to last.
It's not the kind of pain I can deal with when I know that
someone should be there,
And I've found my friend gone and far away and he doesn't
really care.
When I'm not by your side I miss you so bad.
But you just dull your pain with the booze and those other girls
you had.
I hope you find complete peace without all the troubles that
have surrounded you for years,
But please stop blaming me for all the tears.
So now it doesn't matter that I have just been a crutch, that
someone to hold your hand,
I'm going to have to let you go so you can be a man.
I'll look you straight in the eye as I let you go,
Even though you'll try to hurt me, that's something we already
know.
When you look me straight in the eye you don't see me at all,
And even though I'm crying my voice doesn't sound out to you
or call.
Then you'll reach out to hold me but I could barely stand your
touch,
This kind of thing you've called your love for me has been way
too much.
Now I've come to know that I am so much less a part of you,
this caterpillar has grown,

The wiser I've become the more I know this butterfly has flown.
I've broken the jar we've kept me in and I'm flying away from here.
So free I could never remember the fears you own,
That this butterfly has been freed from tears,
Now you're the one alone.

Lisa
1992

WHAT YOU WANT

Till you get what you want,
You don't know what you need.
Till you let it all out,
You don't know how much you can bleed.
When asking is the question,
And the answer is hidden,
Love is the best thing that is not forbidden.
Together we'll look for tomorrow,
Find the love and not the sorrow.
Then we've got what we want,
We got what we need,
No more crying,
We have been freed.

(chorus)

So you get it and you got it baby and that's good.
Love is where the strong have stood.
Now hold it and feel it baby and hang on.
When were together it's never wrong.
Together we're strong.
Together we belong.

Lisa
1994

LIFE IS WRITTEN IN THE DARK

Numbers can be manipulated,
But words can get twisted.
Either either are real . . .
Or never existed.
To have thought on it to long,
May never have been enough.
To have left it alone could only be a bluff.
To pick it back up and play the game,
It's only your mind, sane or insane.
To touch and to feel and to cry human tears,
To reach out for something in the nothing of years,
To hold in your hand the answers inside,
To have made dignity your stand,
Yet . . . to only have died . . .
INTO THE BLACK HOLE

Lisa
April 4, 2001

INTO THE LIFE

I cannot face the grave with this dirt on my face.
I cannot face the earth without existence, a trace.
I can ask for the water to make myself clean.
I can dream of tomorrow if I know what I mean.
I may dip into the washbowl of human desire.
I may cleanse myself being tried by fire.
I may turn around with a snow-white grin.
I may stand before you alive again.
THROUGH THE LIGHT

Lisa
April 4, 2001

LIFE IS WRITTEN IN THE DARK

Numbers can be manipulated,
But words can get twisted.
Either either are real . . .
Or never existed.
To have thought on it to long,
May never have been enough.
To have left it alone could only be a bluff.
To pick it back up and play the game,
It's only your mind, sane or insane.
To touch and to feel and to cry human tears,
To reach out for something in the nothing of years,
To hold in your hand the answers inside,
To have made dignity your stand,
Yet . . . to only have died . . .
INTO THE BLACK HOLE

INTO THE LIFE

I cannot face the grave with this dirt on my face.
I cannot face the earth without existence, a trace.
I can ask for the water to make myself clean.
I can dream of tomorrow if I know what I mean.
I may dip into the washbowl of human desire.
I may cleanse myself being tried by fire.
I may turn around with a snow-white grin.
I may stand before you alive again.
THROUGH THE LIGHT

Lisa
April 4, 2001

SEASONED
AND BASTED
TENDERLY JUICY TASTED
AT THE DINNER HOUR I CENTER PLACE IT
AS A FEAST FOR THE CEMETARY BANQUET
LET THEM SPREAD IT ON A PIECE OF BREAD
AND EAT THE WHOLE THING
WHILE I'M LIEING
DEAD

- - - - - - - - - - - - - - - -
IN HINDSIGHT

Lisa
1994

THE MAD HATTERS' FREEDOM CHILD

Imagination run wild
Crazy child
Lost in the damages of a mind.
Hold your own hand,
Yes, hold it kind
And the silly child won't run wild . . .
Now there are no friends
But you start talking again,
Because the wind will listen for more than awhile . . .
How this crazy life has been the mad Hatters' moonlight trial.
Hung at dawn
From the dark road you were on,
So the end of life's lonely dark mile.
Imagination run wild
And let them be in denial,
For there was never a crazy child,
Only hell on earth,
Where they stole your birth,
And ate all the after too
With a sickly smile.
Imprisoned you away from love its true,
The Mad Hatters' freedom child.

So let them spread it on a piece of bread
And eat some more while you're lying dead.
Seasoned and basted,
Tenderly juicy tasted.
At the dinner hour
I've center placed it,
As the last feast for the cemetery banquet.
Let the birds of heaven become many
And no, leave no not any . . .
No flesh or bone, of those whom so joyfully have shown themselves
Thankful to be alive this day.
My blood for me does pray

Lisa

That justice will not delay
To exact the full price
For the Mad Hatter's treasure,
Done dirty and buried.
So measure for measure
For each weight she carried
To let them pay up their bill,
For the guilty pleasure
Of their own fresh kill . . .
For the Mad Hatters' freedom child.

Lisa September 9, 2007

AN ANGELS' QUEST

An angels' quest is as a surefooted pursuer to reclaim the souls
Embracing coldness with an icy interest.
Still some become like fireflies in a windstorm,
Being swayed dizzily in a corkscrewed rush with neither direction nor vision.
Descending upon those palely illuminated,
From far beyond the black forest of poverty and misery,
Comes the strange boned, malevolent, malignant, sharp and dark adversary.
In his sharpened promenade, pierced by their succulent confusion tasted,
He releases the wrought-iron gravity latch to his iron-railed iron gate.
Quickly gathering the sour and sulfurous nauseating stench of decomposing flesh, mind and
Soul.
Scrap.
Shadows motionless, desperately seeking the safe and true passageway through the
Windstorm.
And unseen dangers have triggered recollection of awareness.
An angel did come speaking softly and kindly of the ominous brilliance of Jehovah God,
Christ and his light.
An Angel did come.

Lisa
1996

DOOR BELLS

You wanted someone who would never turn away.
I always wanted someone who would never let me go.
You wanted that one who would stay.
If it was love I wanted to know.
We stood in the doorway yet we never said goodbye.
We heard the bells still no one asked the other why.
As we look at each other . . .
Man, child and mother . . .
Letting go of one another.
Though we know we may never hear those bells again,
Still, we cry each and every time they end,
"Oh please Jehovah answer the door,
Let me love my family once more? "

Lisa
(Of course it was the year_____)

AT THE GOOD LORDS' INN

Everybody was moving through the house,
Yet none could be found.
Though somebody was beside them,
We all looked around.
So many rooms have been filled,
As each life was thrilled to have come to roam . . .
Such a big happy home.
As each one tried a new door,
They laid behind them a brand floor.
A space to provide
A new home for a heart inside.
No one cried as we all came through the door to Gods'
house.
The Good Lords' Inn . . .
Where he's beside you my friend.
Where he hopes you will seek to find that behind his door,
Lay a brand new floor to mankind.
Where we all walk together,
Where the lights always shine.
We're all an open door of the almighty shrine.

Lisa
1991

Lisa

JEHOVAH GOD IN HEAVEN

Jehovah God in heaven,
Angels above,
Love us,
Keep us,
Fill us with love.
Stay by us,
Guide us,
With peace like the dove.
Lord love us,
And help us through.
Beside us,
In light of the things we do.
You love us,
You cover us,
You believe in us too.

Lisa
1999

BETWEEN JEHOVAH AND ME

I see they are coming after me.
I see they wanted more than they need.
I see they can't find what's inside.
I see I don't need to try and hide.
Never mind yeah, what they don't see.
Never mind yeah, just let it be.
It's between Jehovah and me.
I don't need to ask no questions.
I don't need to wonder why.
I just need babe, that's all I cry.
I don't wonder what for.
I don't ask those kind of questions anymore.
I find all I need at Jehovah Gods' door.
It's open between God and me.

Lisa
1999

Lisa

YES GOD LOVES YOU DEAR

Please take me away from hear I pray.
Can you take me away?
Can you fly me from here today?
Please hold me near.
Lift me up inside.
Give me a place to hide.
Dry my tears.
Put your wings around me.
Love me as you found me.
Take away my fears.
Yes God loves you dear.

Lisa
2000

RAINBOW AND THE ARK

A rainbow that breaks the heavens at the sunset of the day,
Opens peace from heaven,
Jesus Christ is king this day.
Let us break bread; kneel and pray.
With our hearts and heads skyward,
Our words by the word,
As our souls believing hear of the great fear inspiring day of
Jehovah.
As sure as the eagles shall soar skyward,
Our souls believing in the truth we hear,
Choosing to live our lives by the word,
Know without any fear that we shall never die.
The Lord God Jehovah adored,
Our children will never cry.
Though it shall be evening it shall never be dark,
As promised, as promise as the rainbow and the ark.

Lisa
1999

UNITY

If someone could change the past,
Change what's been done to you at last.
But we all know without Jehovah God it will never be,
Even though you keep trying to open the eyes that may never
see.
When I look at you I don't see a color,
I see an undeniable strength,
Expression of patience,
A constant vigil from one race and no other . . .
There is unity . . .
In the race for life amongst Gods' people there is you and me.
Jehovah is true humanity, true unity.

Lisa
1999

A DRINK FROM THE WELL

Bow your head inside your own heart,
Even though it may feel as if it's been torn apart,
It's become easy to cry for each other, for one another.
You can count on the tears of your heart to form a full-bodied soul,
Like raindrops fill the bodies of water.
They are not without purpose,
And go with full force against everything in the pathway,
They are leaving nothing and no one thirsty, agape love.

Lisa
1994

Lisa

THE DAY

There is a day to come,
It seems long in waiting.
Anxious hearts, anticipating . . .
No pain inside,
No tears we cry,
The day of you and I.
As Jesus Christ does reign,
The anointed follow his train,
And Jehovah God rules from above,
So the earth is filled with love.
No more death or disease.
No more living on our knees.
They will have lifted us up to stand,
And brought peace to all man.
That day that is to come,
Has followed Gods' glorious son.
He has kingdom rule
And brings an end to the wicked fool
Who refuses to obey.
The law was set forth by Jehovah,
The day of you and I,
No pain inside,
No tears we cry.

Lisa
1989 – 2006

WHY ASK Y

Y—No Peace?
Y—No Love?
Y—No Justice?

Y—Lose Hope?

Why then, the only Y left would be at the end of
TragedY.

Lisa
1995

THE PAIN

When morning comes that I might sleep it in,
I think of God and what I mean to him.
He knows I hurt and feel bad inside.
How much could I take?
How much I have cried.
All Jehovah wants is for me to be pain free.
And he hates the sickness caused by Satan's misery.
So each morning I crawl right out of bed,
And take the pain my body dreads.
For Jehovah I make a stand,
And get my rest the best I can.
With this Jehovah helps me.
When it is I hurt to him I plea
Your kingdom come and an end to Satan's misery!
Be still the pain so deep inside.
It's so you hurt me till I have cried.
Yet laugh and play and run I will.
Beyond the pain . . . Jehovah my spirit fill,
With life and love and happiness,
To overcome and do my best
Against pain and sickness that crouch before me.
Through all I live to Jehovah's glory.

Lisa
2001

A ROCK

Like a rock wedged in sand . . .
I long to be swept by the tide to another shore.
The world has stoned me.
HEAVY!
But I am bigger than any grain of sands.
Solidity must fall where it lands.
Gravity,
Longevity,
Hardened strength are my core.
A body of earth and water . . .
I stand diligently upon the shore.

Lisa
July 199

LUCINDA MEADOWS

Loose in the meadows,
Loose in the sky,
Lucinda sings her songs for Jehovah God.
Lucinda loves him,
And she always prays.
She knows he answers her in his own special way.
Lucinda weeps and she wonders why,
There is so much suffering under pretty blue skies.
But she doesn't blame God because that would not be fare or true.
She knows Satan is the reason for suffering, Lucinda's too.
Loose in the meadows,
Loose in the sky,
Lucinda sings her songs and cries.
She prays for man and Gods' kingdom to come,
So all Gods' children may laugh and have fun.
Beneath his majestic mountains'
Across his beautiful planes,
Lucinda knows without Gods' kingdom,
There is no peace for earth again.
Loose in the meadows,
Loose in the sky,
Lucinda sings of her hopes to Jehovah God.
They talk of the time when death will be gone,
And sickness won't harm; not any one.
They speak of the future in peace for all mankind,
And they set out together to seek that this you will find,
Loose in the meadows,
Loose in the sky,
They search for each of you . . .
So you won't die.
Lucinda Meadows,
Lucinda Sky,
Please sing with Lucinda?
Please won't you try?
Let's pray for Jehovah's kingdom to come

Through Christ Jesus his son.
Pray for his kingdom blessing to come each day,
And before long our prayers will be answered just that way,
Loose in the meadows,
Loose in the sky,
We will all sing our songs to Jehovah God.

Lisa
1995 – 2007

Lisa

LITTLE ONE

It's OK if you want to have some fun little one.
It's OK if you are dreaming of the sun little one.
It's more than just a dream today,
Where children can step out and play,
Where laughter is the way little one.
You're all right—you're OK little one.

You are all right, you're OK.
You should have wings babe that could fly away,
And your friends could fly by your side,
Where you can safely play and not hide little one.
Butterflies in the wind have a really cool ride little one.

It's OK. It's OK. It's all right, It's OK.
Pretty little wings to fly you away,
Somewhere far from a disturbed world of fear,
Where it is natural for little children to be here.
It's OK. It's OK. It's all right, It's Ok.

Just imagine the change into God's new world,
Where freedom and laughter belong to every boy and girl,
Just taking off in flight,
Use your sight,
With all of your might little one,
You won't need to be in fright
Your wings are going to feel the flight,
Where it's OK, It's all right little one.
Jehovah God promised us a paradise, little one, where you'll
be OK,
You'll be all right little one.
God does not lie; he has taken the time to show you that
caterpillars can fly.
Butterflies don't cry little one.
They just believe there is a sky little one.
It will soon be OK,
It will soon be alright little one.

It's OK. It's OK. It's alright little one.
It's OK. It's OK. It's alright little one.
(CHORUS)

Lisa
1996-2007

SOLDIERS' SOUL, KILLER HERO
(Jeff Lucey (Died 2006) another Man Of Millions)

His eyes are crying
Because he saw those dying by the end of his gun.
But those tears are shying from coming down his face,
That's how it is when asked to kill the human race.
You can't see the guilty murderers' plea . . .
When really he is begging "Please Kill Me"!
You have to look deep into the eyes that are crying
Because he saw those dying by his enemies' gun.
Child or soldier
Nothing feels colder
Than the bullets flying.
The blood never drying
Under the hot earth sun.
All terrains are different
But every human race the same.
Both sides hell bent
For their countries bloody war game.
A HERO for the Cause!!!
The killer of us all!!!
His eyes are crying.
In the mission there is no denying
You soldier soul.
You can't pick or choose whose living or dying
Before the Killer Hero.
As his soul begs and pleads . . .
There is not THE,
There is only OUR and WE!
It's not 'The Soldiers Soul'
Or 'The Killer Hero'.
It was 'OUR' war when I was socially manipulated to sign up
that day.
It was 'WE' fight for something 'WE' believe, before I found out
the hard way that
Killing was not the way.

It was 'OUR' Soldiers and 'United WE Stand' before I found
out that I am the 'ONE'
Left with blood on my hands!!!!!!!
Now what have I 'ONE' soldier laments . . . for the 'WE' and
'OUR' never went to kill . . .
Too kill by the gun with eyes wide open to blow the brains out
of someone.
For I am 'The Soldier Soul',
'THE KILLER HERO'!
So please forgive me my father and my sweet mother
If I feel I must go?
For 'THEY' taught me "I" 'Cain', kill my brother.
Now I feel a need for some kind of rest for my soul . . .
A peaceful sleeping death.
I see no other way out of a world so hell bent on taking away
every 'ONES' breath.

"I" Die Alone,
'Army of 'ONE'.
I'd live and die for you all
But crying is no fun.
So for me they gave me no other game,
So I, "Soldier Soul, Your Killer Hero" let go of my remorse and
my unending pain.

Jeff Lucey killed himself.

Lisa (Empathy: your pain in my heart)
2006

I once heard a line said that could never be more true. I don't know who came up with it
but I heard it on 06-13-07. Quote . . ."Love lies buried beneath the pen and ink that writes it"
It reminds me of a poem I wrote back in 1986 that I had given away but I believe it goes
something like this . . .

PAPER THE STAGE

Pencil this is your page and through life, love, unhappiness, and rage this will be your stage.
Take with you your eraser to dance with my dear.
Whatever you find in your heart you may write it here.
An in the end if you are left with a broken heart and nothing left to say,
Maybe your sweet eraser could erase all the sorrow that you were engaged in,
Maybe you could paper the stage then.
Maybe what you write could be erased away and no one will know the feelings behind
all those tears or know of your sad dance through all the years.
Pencil and eraser . . . the page is your stage and its' dance are your tears . . . if only you could
erase away all your sorrowful years.

Lisa
1986 –2007

IT"S JUST LIFE

Remember the road we took,
Remember the life taken,
Remember the choices we made,
Left our heart breaking.
Remember the times of wine,
The laughter, the fun and sunshine.
Try to remember the times as kind.
Remember the road is never really left behind.
Remember the bridges crossed.
Remember that games are either won or lost,
Someone had to pay the cost
To remember our dreams,
The life we've taken.
Remember the rock and roll soul shaken.
Remember the lovemaking.
Remember the stars making our eyes twinkle in the light.
Remember the road taken.
The life taken doesn't matter if we're perfect at trying to get it
right,
And all we can do is try.
So why not try a little harder to not let it get you down.
Remember its' just life.

(Chorus)
It's just life . . .
It's just life . . .
It's just life . . .
I'll be with you in life.
You'll be alright . . .
You'll feel alive.
It's just life.

Lisa
2006

SHALL WE DANCE

All the world is a stage
In this great tirade
Beautifully brutal provision called life.
As we circle full in our stand
And we hold on to one another, hand in hand:
Brother, sister, father, mother, child, woman or man.
Shall we curtsey,
Or bow,
Sep 1, Step 2, but how?
Oh howl in life's' ballroom grand!
Look in the eyes but can't believe,
And then watch the others turn and leave.
The swing of life's' pendulum goes back and forth
And life, love and dilemma have taken their course.
But out to the side
Or step back in.
Better swallow your pride with a snow-white grin.
We're doing the family dance of bitter sin.
In all the world, in a sadistic stage,
We dance to the mad hatter's silent rage, in a laughing cry.
It's the tragically, tyrannical, brutal tirade
That life was made and so was I.

Am I glad we had this dance?
It was just chance meeting you here today.
Shall we dance?

Lisa
2007

A GOLDEN TICKET

He's giving away a golden ticket to be by his side,
Who'll be the winner of the golden ticket he cried.
A ticket to the future,
A ticket for fame,
A ticket for love,
And to carry his name.
A golden ticket of dreams and all precious things,
A ticket to ride,
Yes she's got a ticket to ride is what he sings.
A ticket to step into the light and let everyone see
The kind of woman a golden ticket winner would be.
She'll wear silver and gold,
All diamonds and pearls,
The finest designers and threads of the world.
The most glorious of homes
In any place on the earth.
All fabulous cars for whatever they're worth.
She'll jet set the continents and his children give birth.
She's got a ticket to ride, a golden ticket to the whole earth.
He's got a golden ticket but she must be a golden-hearted girl,
For only a good man would give her the world.
He sang out the news around the globe,
A golden ticket is what I hold,
I have a golden ticket, he cries.
Why can't I find her here right before my eyes?

A golden-hearted girl sits all alone and she does cry . . .
She says I got two tickets to paradise but no one here by my side.
Where is a love like pure gold in this world for me to hold?
I don't need anything but him and God please before I'm old?
I just need to be warm in his arms because alone I am so cold.
A golden hearted girl for a good, good man.

Lisa

I know I will find him someday holding my hand.
That's all I'll ever need to help me stand.
I've sat so long waiting,
I've stopped debating the kind of girl he thinks I am.
I can only do the best I can.
I take my heart in prayer to Jehovah God . . .
And he said if you have love, trust, and faith in him, and in me
you have two tickets to see
paradise.
A golden hearted girl sits all alone and she cries . . . I got two
tickets to paradise.
Why can't I find him right here before my eyes?

Lisa
2006

HONEY DO LIST

Honey do you think you can get a few things done for me
today?
Honey do you think that'll be OK?
Honey do you mind?
>Well honey I'll try to be so kind.
>Honey can you wait a minute do you mind?
>Honey, it's almost the end of the game and
>The chiefs are going to take the super bowl this time.
Honey do you realize the bottom step on that porch has waited
months now?
Honey do you see the house shutters have fallen down?
Honey do you think you can unplug the back toilet today?
Honey do you see your daughter wants to play?
>Honey I know you need me
>And I'll be glad to get right to it
>You'll see,
>Now honey could you get me a beer?
>And honey take these potato chips back to the kitchen
>you hear?
Honey do you think I'm your maid?
Honey do you think you married you a personal slave?
Honey do you see the list of things needing done?
Honey do you plan to get to just one?
I've cooked and cleaned and done all you asked.
Honey do you plan to get to just one task?
>Honey do you think I'm blind?
>Honey do you forget in so quick a time?
>Honey do you remember how I held you tight last night?
>Through the thunder and the rain?
>Honey do you remember how much my check was,
>Cause I can't remember a thing?
Honey do you even really want to go there?
Honey do you know how hard it is for three kids to bare?
Honey do you think soccer and dance classes come for free?
Oh Sweet Honey do you really think it's cheap to look as good
as me?

Honey do you think I'm not happy to give you ever
Penny I've got to spare?
Honey do you plan to want to take another vacation trip this
Year?
Honey do you think I better start to save?
Or honey do you already got the road paved?
Honey do you think there will be stars out tonight?
Honey do you think you will be alright or will you be alone?
Honey do you think the dog will move over?
Honey do you think your next women will be a real rover?
Honey do you think my bark is bigger than my bite?
Oh Sweet Honey, do you really want this honey do list
To end us in a fight?
Honey do you think for us as a family that's going to
be right?
Honey do you really mean it when you say you'll get to doing
the 'To Do List' today?
Honey do you realize I just want a little something done?
Honey do you understand you're the only one?
Honey do you think there is anything more that I could
want to Be?
Than the one you my honey do need?
Honey do you really love me so?
Honey do you think I can make this up to you somehow?
Honey do you see that our love really does grow?
Honey do you think I'm acting better now?
Honey do you think you could give me your kiss?
Honey do you think we could share a hug
Before I get to the honey do list?
Honey don't you dare try to scurry away.
Honey you know the first thing you need to do
Is make love to me today.
Honey Do, Honey DEW!
Did my sweet honey do her list today?

Lisa
2007

HELL HATH NO FURY

Hell hath no fury like a women scorned,
So if I had my way you'd never been born.
The heart of a women angels fear to tread,
They're afraid they'll find another no good man dead.
It really could have been all just water under the bridge,
If that would have just turned out to be either of us brand of beer in the fridge.
Looks like that bridge may finally get crossed.
But since you did it with another dame it's your life it's going to cost.
Don't tell me I'm getting out of hand!
You just don't like our new set up game plan.
Now let's really play follow the leader,
Let's see what is good and best for the cheater.
In this house you were suppose to be a man,
Since that didn't work out, like many of your paychecks,
I guess again I'll have to do what I can.
Play the Ships' Captain on deck and lay down the law.
Looks like you'll be walking the plank after all.
Don't worry baby I'll never kiss and tell,
But since you chose the pirates booty and not the queen's gold,
Watch your step because a woman's' heart can be turned cold.
You thought you'd never be found out like the oceans' secrets,
But with what we got left between us let's see what the sharks get?
Because hell hath no fury like a women scorned,
And you're going to wish you'd never been born.
Angels won't go where men fear to tread,
But then again angels no better than to climb into another woman's bed.

Lisa
2007

Lisa

PSYCHEDELIC BLUES

Running out of time
Can't get you off my mind,
And I need your love.
Running through this life blind,
Because I find no time to unwind and sit down beside my
love.
We can fly,
We can try for the sky.

Twisting and turning,
Got the floor burning,
With the hard rockers song,
And all the peoples dance along.
All the peoples dance along.
To the jazzy beat – hip-hop jumping – black beat thumping
psychedelic blues,
Hard rocking straight through,
Straight through you,
Cause the boys got the jumping jazzy beat.
Hip-hop jumping black beat thumping psychedelic blues.
Rocking straight through you and I.
We can dance
In the dark of the day,
With the curtains drawn,
Me and my baby just want to play.
In the dark of the day were having it on. Rock On. Rock ON.
To that jazzy beat hip hop jumping, black beat thumping,
psychedelic blues.
Hard rocking, Hard rocking, Hard rocking psychedelic blues,
Rock On, Rock On.

Lisa
2006

CRAZY FAN

I was just standing there wondering how I'd get tickets
With no money in hand and my job on the picket?
Then I heard them giving them away on the radio.
8th caller in line plus airline tickets to go.
Ma Bell must have owed me one to have shut off all other lines,
Otherwise, how could I have been the 8th caller just right on time?
Stuff like that just doesn't happen for me.
I screamed all my excitement to Wolf man Jack on the phone!
Wolf man Jack said, "I'm no mind reader little girl, but you sound like a crazy lady, I
Bet you live alone."
I was going to give out two tickets, but you're probably going to go it on your own.
Am I right?
That really hurt me. I took it very personal inside,
So I said, "No, because I thought I'd be seeing you tonight."
Wolf man said, "I'll call the cops if I can't mail these to you, right?"
So what I get excited, I'm just a fan, and then I cried.
Wolf man Jack said, "That's right, but I hope not one of mine, I think your brain might be fried."
So two days later I finally dried my tears and my depression passed away,
Because I got my ticket in the mail and I'm on my way.

(chorus)
Crazy fan that's what I am,
I do agree, and my eight friends I keep inside of me.
Crazy fan for the star far out of my league
But that star's bound to like one of the others inside of me.

And there I was at the arena gate,
Soon for early but far from late

Lisa

With just enough time to janitor the halls:
All three floors, the roof and the grounds – I'll cover it all!
I'll locate where my star comes in, where my star dresses, and
where he leaves.
I'm just a fan . . . and for my star I have needs!
We all have needs:
Jan has needs, Betty's heart bleeds and Alice wants him to
fall down the rabbit hole
And still the queen is yelling for his head off don't you know.

(chorus)
Crazy fan that's what I am,
I do agree, and so does my eight friends I keep inside of me.
Crazy fan for my star not so far now out of my league,
I know he's bound to love one of me.

But back to reality,
Its stage presence time,
All the lights are out and the crowds feeling fine.
Where is he my fan?
There he is! My Star, my man!!
The audience has sent out a deafening applause!
Yes! He is definitely all there is and all there ever was!
Oh the show is so good!
Oh the show is so great!
Oh how blessed I am to have got through the gate!
Just yesterday I had nothing and going nowhere in sight!
Now here I am with my star and my star is with me tonight!
He knows I have needs,
Like an autograph across the picture I'll take when down on
his knees.
And then a touch, a kiss, and an invitation to dinner please?
Towards the end of the show I guess I'll slip down the isle
It's just straight from the 3rd floor balcony to the ground floor,
Hardly a ½ mile.
To be quick about it I'll just swing down from the chandelier.
Drop down behind the drums so not to make a scene.
To the crowd just another rock and roll stunt in air,

But to my star he'll love the fact that I'm here.
I'll just watch the rest of the show,
I'll hardly be seen.
Now wait just a minute!!
Why do these bruisers got to be so mean!
I just want to be close that's all I'm about!
Then after the show I can follow him out.
Oh no man, you've ticked off Diane!
Girl will knock you out!
Now I guess I'll have to disappear into the flow.
That's all right because I know he'll be leaving by the back door.

(chorus)
I'm just your crazy fan! That's all I am!
I'm just your crazy fan. I'm only doing what I can to be near you!
The better just to hear you my dear!
I know you're mad they pushed me away, and I know you really want me here to stay!
We can go for a walk and have a little talk about how dear I am to you.
I'll be so happy to hear you say it to the world . . . never was there a more beautiful girl
Whose love and loyalty are for you! Never was there a truer fan to adore too!
I'm just your crazy fan that's all I am!
So slide over in the limo Hun, there is eight of me not just one.
That just makes having you a crazy fan a whole lot more fun.
"Drive on James.
Isn't that right babe?"
"That's right James, take us home."

Lisa
2004

NOW GO AWAY

I don't want you.
I don't need you.
I don't love you.
Go Away.
You're not my kind
Too help me unwind.
I don't want you.
I don't need you.
I don't love you.
Now go away.

I've got my mind set on sunshine.
I won't let you shroud me in your dark cloud,
So go away.
All my rainbows
Are what my love shows,
And there's no rain to cause me pain from the one I love.
I don't want you.
I don't need you.
I don't love you.
So I'm sorry – but – go away.
Maybe you can't take it,
But someone will come to help you make it through another
day.
All my prayers are that you will find a love that's true.
Somewhere you can stay,
So just for me and mine, can't you just let us be fine?
Cause I don't want you.
I don't need you.
I don't love you.
You've got to go away.

Lisa
April 28, 2006

JUST TO BLEED

Everybody just wants to be somebody.
Nobody wants to be forgot,
And nobody likes anybody who tries to be something they are not.
From the seat of power
To the street of the pauper,
There is something we all need,
For everybody to remember were only human and not alive just to bleed.
So take me in your arms and hold me in your heart.
Remember the ending is just a beginning for someone else to start.
Everybody just wants to be somebody.
Nobody wants to be forgot
Everybody wants to play a role but nobody knows the part.
From the seat of power
To the street of the pauper,
To fill an insatiable need . . .
Too not be alive just to bleed.
Alive just to bleed,
Just to bleed,
Just to bleed,
Just to bleed.

Lisa
2005-2007

INSANITARIUM SANCTUARY

One day at a time.
So you sit down beside the water
Though the moons shining the sun's rising.
Time is always passing.
But the sunrise is always asking you to call it a new day.

But it's not a new day.
It's the same as it ever was.
It's the same as yesterday.
It's the same as it ever was.
Janis Joplin once said, "As everybody knows out on the plane
It's all the same day man".
Same as it ever was . . .
See the girl crying in the window . . .
See the girl crying in the window . . .
See the girl crying in the window . . .
See the girl crying in the window . . .
See the girl crying in the window . . .
See the girl crying in the window . . .
See the girl crying in the window . . .
See the girl crying in the window . . .
See the girl crying in the window . . .
See the girl crying in the window . . .
See the window . . . the girl is crying,
In her sanctuary . . . insane—itarium.
Sanitarium . . . the same as it ever was.

Lisa
July 8, 1967-July 8, 2007

THE UNFATHOMABLE LOVE

With tears and sorrow
That crouch down tomorrow
And fall from my eyes.
From dreams of mere gladness
Washed down in sadness
And swallowed like pills.
My body is ill.
My mind is still.
And my heart is deaf and dumb,
That I am the one . . .
Who could believe in unfathomable love.
Why did I ever dream of you and me?
Why do I think that life we can live and breathe?
When nothing ever comes but the fears shot by guns,
And the rainy clouds to cover the fun.
Why did I dream that what would be,
Would be some kind of happiness between you and me?
When love is in the graves
And no human gets saved from war.
The toy soldiers are sent
On the thought that they went
On unfathomable love.
But they find themselves on their knees . . .
"Oh God I'm begging . . . please don't let me die,
Cause I
Got more dreams than this mistaken one it seems?
Why, why, why?"
I'm sure I believe there will be something left for you and me.
I'll swear and I stand
For taking your hand,
That promises lead to true happy days,
And Gods righteous ways
Of unfathomable love.
And when I get home you won't be alone, I'll be there.

All that is good but it' misunderstood in funeral attire.

Lisa

The message is sent but the letter got bent on a broken wire.
Dot, dot, dash, dash, dot, dot never got through.
I don't know which end sent it but mother and son are gone.
It was in the morning dew of the dawn.
Now there is nothing to do for dreams unseen by anyone but
unfathomable love . . .
The unfathomable love of Jehovah.

Lisa
2002

LOVE AT DAWN

Midnight roses
My family poses
For a love song.
Champaign visions
In bubbled derisions
Of memories so strong.
Dreaming to music
And love beyond.
Sleeping as we sleep
In lilies of the pond.
Love forever
Love at dawn.

Lisa
1996

THE LEGEND

A legend never knows
Where it came from
Or where it will go.
It lives by trial and error.
It's tried by fire and swears
That it will last longer than you and I.

A legend begins with a dream.
One that comes way down from you and me,
It tells no lies.
It only cries of time gone by . . .
The bravest times of you and I.

A legend sometimes screams
From way beyond life and human dreams.
Seems like walking through lonesome nights,
But in the dark somehow a trick of light,
And love is on its mind.
The legend that love has left behind.

It's told from one to the other.
Strange tales of passion, madness, desire and a lover.
It shrouds in mystery
And covers in the veil of life.
It weds through history
A man and his wife.

A legend the soul has laid
Of love and life where two are one and dreams are made,
To walk through time the endless mile,
The legend of love
Where hearts run wild,

And by creation has come a child . . .
A legend is born.

Lisa
November 15, 2004

Written for my grandbaby on the way 11-15-04
Andrew Cole Erickson was born on 06-03-05 to Nicholas Jason Erickson and Lisa Marie
Stubble.

Lisa

SCHADENFREUDE

Oh for the one who writes their heart out.
Tells the whole world of their fears and doubt.
Just as the blood, so would the ink dare spill,
Every little tidbit of the swallowed bitter pill.
Oh for the one whose hearts upon stage
Living all emotions from love to rage.
A simple glance in the mirror
Might have told the truth.
That it wouldn't have been any clearer had you sold your own
tickets at the booth.
A small price they pay to see you play.
Woe for you that they have dared not know
Just for them you had to give them your soul.
Oh for the one now seen upon stage center screen,
How what a marvelous life it all did seem.
No star in the sky shown as bright as all this.
Yet for all that life had only need of one true kiss.
Oh for the one does fame call by thy name,
A sacrificial sheep for the entertainment game.
Now dance for us,
Now play for us,
Now sing.
Now act out thy sorrows
And awards we will bring.
Write it all down for us,
The whole thorny crown for us,
And pose for the camera please.
And never, no never fall off the high wire trapeze.
It will then be front-page news.
How you got a new hat, new boat, new car, and new shoes.
The brand name of these items and the price tag you must
share.
Never forgetting we're critiquing each clothing article you wear.
Never break down in front of us please.
It won't do you any good since we've all been convinced this
is a life of ease.

Oh for the one who cannot cry who shared all their pain.
Though they gave you everything
It's not the same.
In privately imprisoned in the peoples cage,
Just another person with needs but bleeds it out on the world's stage.
Oh for you, who really do want all of this
Who swear you don't care,
But are found sitting there in front of the TV
Laughing at, but wishing you could be a star and be seen.
Wanting if nothing else but to give your star a kiss.
On the worlds stage you like to act like you're so different, but almost just the same.
Poor you, you're not getting paid . . . your horrific terrific star rising never came.

Lisa
2000

COLD BLUE

How will you ever walk in those shoes?
Do you know how to hold on to those deep down cold as hell blues?
What makes you think you can measure up?
Will you even know how to drink from the same poison cup?
The bitter cup of loneliness,
The glitter and glamour are just for the show, yes,
But those shoes are a whole other thing.
Step up—Belt them out—Hit them with the rock-n-roll blues sing.
You don't take those steps lightly in those shoes.
Don't walk so softly through the news daily blues.
What size can they be?
How big do you see?
Do you need to step back?
Or should you run up the hill like Jill and Jack?
They come tumbling down after all.
They took their fall.
These are the shoes that step hardly light through the broken heart of the blues.
Many came before and many will come after.
And many will feel the madness of the laughter and wish they never came,
To have walked in the shoes of the blues name of fame.
It's going to leave you cold blue.
Cold blue.

Lisa
2007

CRAZY HORSE

What's in the thunder
Screaming through the wind,
Heard through the lightning
As earths ground touches heaven again?
Sitting Bull . . . an earthling man
Saw the child crying for his mother again.
What's in the sky
That talks to you,
That lights up just why
The child's so blue?
His father is loud in a war crying rain.
Painted horses run proud
For Cherokee pain,
Apache will come, Comanche and Sioux,
On the mad ride for Crazy Horse son,
To white man his justice due.
So many hides found on rattle back trail.
The train glistens like a long sleek black snake beneath the
moon,
As the rails rattle the rattlers tune.
The rustlers and outlaws rotted in Buffalo Canyon
The day the sun set on the white man, and blood was the
moon.

Lisa
2000 – 2007

HELP ME (SONG)

(Begins with sounds of fire trucks, sirens blaring, footsteps heading up the stairs toward the apartment, and a knock on the door. *"Mam, Mam. We're here to help, can you hear us? Is there anyone there?"***) She opens the door and begins to sing:**

Help.
Help me I'm all alone.
Help me I'm on my own.
There is no one else.
No one could ever tell all the things that I've been through since life began. (Knock, knock. *"Fire Department! Fire Department!"***)**
Help. Help. I'm reaching out for you.
I need to know if you're reaching out for me too.
I need to know if your one I could trust.
I need that promise between the two of us.
Help.
Help me understand.
Will you be my hero?
Help.
Save me from my mind.
Show me you can be kind.
I've felt the abuse of others before.
I've hoped for better and got nothing more.
I've dreamed big to be crushed so small.
I feel so much sorrow and still no one answers the call.
Help. (Sounds of helicopters and sirens blaring. Her voice says:
Help me. *"What are you doing?"* **She tries to beat on the windows**
And doors. *"Wait! Wait!"***)**
Help to knock down the door of this misery.
Please come to rescue me.
(*"Mam, mam. We need you to help yourself"***)**

God knows I've tried.
Is there no one else?
Help, I feel so alone.
Why is sadness all I've ever known?
Help.
Please comfort me.
Hold me close so I won't bleed.
(The ambulance paramedics have arrived by this time. *"We have a pulse. The bleeding is under control but we're going to need the life flight!"***)**
Help . . .
Help me hang on.
Will you help me to figure out why life can go so wrong?
Why can't love come to me?
Help me get strong with a future that I can see.
Just like you I want a happy life.
I'd like a family to love on beautiful summer nights.
Why is my home in misery, it isn't right?
Please help.
Please help me . . . (Piano solo)
Tell me tomorrow is there for me.
(Paramedic says; *"We're losing her! We're losing her! C'mon! C'mon! Fight! Hang in there. You got people who care.***)**
What will be there for me?
I need reason and hope to go on.
I need help . . . help from someone.
Help! Help! Please help me!
Tell me who will come for me?
Who will walk this earth here beside me?
Who will help me to be happy beneath all the hopeful sunshine?

(Whispers in melody)
So today I got too lost deep in the lonely misery of my mind.

That is where I came to live so it would be hard for you to reach me or come to find . . .
The lack of love leaves no memories to last.
No need to help now the time for love has passed.
By your side you have a hand . . . hold it with the other for your whole life and see if you can be strong alone . . . I've done the best I can. It's the life I've known.
  (Sound of a flat line monitor)

Lisa
2009

ALKEY EYES
(SONG, HAS A SMASHING PUMPKIN SOUND)

You know it ain't fare when you know . . . that every time you turn around everything just blows.

I wish someone would tell me
I wish someone would tell me
I wish someone would tell me
An easy way to work out my life

You try to turn over a new leaf on another day in some new place.
But for all your cost and effort it just blows up in your face.

I wish someone could tell me
I wish someone could tell me
I wish someone could tell me
An easy way to work out my life

I know I was born with this fifth generation disease.
I try to view it as if I need to move along like I were in a wheelchair.
But this is the disease where you fall down because a bottle was sitting there.

I wish someone could help me
I wish someone could help me
I wish someone could help me
With an easier way to work out my life

I didn't fall down from Muscular Dystrophy.
But I wish there was a Jerry working on what I need.
No one ever said it was going to be a life of ease.
But I wish someone would just please
I wish someone would just please
I wish someone would just please
Close up the over abundance of liquor stores in front of me.

Lisa

Because I really need an easier way
I need an easier way
I need an easier way
To work out my life

They say there's a war on drugs but not on me.
The only way they know to help is take away my keys.
Then I see those MAD women standing in the liquor store line
Pheining on that Holiday liquor like a crack head on his last dime
It's ok mamma, you know you're welcome here any time
If something bad happens you probably got the money to buy your way out of your crime
Just like you could afford your own bill in the lobby line
But I sure wish you could tell me
I sure wish you could tell me
Maybe you should tell me
Was that the easiest way you could find to help me work out my life of crime.
Was there really no other way
No other way
Really no other way you could find to help an already troubled mind?

You know it aint fare when every time you turn around this crime of a disease blows a point five.
Thank God I have MAD women out to save lives.
But I wish someone
I really wish someone
Just someone could trade shoes
And then you could just tell me
You could just tell me
You could really be able to tell me
What it's like to be born to have such bad news.
We could start an Alky Eyes organization to help out a little more

Have a bill passed that closes down at least fifty of the hundred thousand liquor stores.
But for the love of
Yes for the love of
I mean for the love of liquor money they'll never recognize
You can get as mad as you want till you bleed red out your eyes
But don't fail to be surprised when you get no where
It's just like having a disease your entire life.

Lisa

LET HIM DOWN

Girl he's got the whole world praying
That you're going to be staying,
But if you got to let him down
Let him down easy.

He's a hard working man, brings home his hard earned pay,
But if you got to let him go, don't you do it that way.
If you got to let him down,
You've got to let him down easy.

When he woke you up this morning you kissed him goodbye,
When you know women that good loving puts the tears in a
man's eyes.
Don't go out that way.
You know what I'm trying to say.
If you've got to let your man down,
You've got to let him down easy.
You've got to,
You've just got to.
You've got to let him down easy.

A man knows life for a woman is rough.
And if love is ever going to work she has got to be tough.
They've got to walk side by side.
They've got to share all the bumps that come with the ride.
They've got to share the rhythm and God knows the blues.
They've got to be the rock,
And know when to roll too.

They've got to hold one another,
Know the real score.
They've got to love one another and keep wanting more.
They've got to realize just what they have deep inside.
Through this cruel world they have got a place to hide.
And they've got to know they are each other's best friend.
So girl if it comes . . .

You thinking it should end.
Please remember woman,
He is your man . . . he is your best friend.
If sure you're going to go out some better way,
Then you've got to know he's got the whole world praying.
If you just got to go,
Let him down easy.
You've just got to find your way to let him down easy.
If you got to get away,
Let him down easy.
Girl, please let your man down easy.

Lisa
October 14, 2004

Lisa

MAKE BELIEVE

Make believe you really love me and that
you'll always be there.
Make believe you are my husband that you'll always care.
Make believe your arms are around me in the
memories we share,
And make believe that love has found me,
a broken heart spared.
We'll make believe that all is good in a world so fair.
Let's make believe we have a good life and children to care,
And make believe I am your wife, who will never be shared,
And make believe in love and romance that dances on air.
In your arms you have found me,
in our eyes no sorrow we bare.
Your tender touch all around me, for the passion of all love is
there.
And hold me closer to your body and to the warmth of your
touch,
And make believe that all is good in the world and the truth
won't hurt so much.
If you can't believe then watch me baby, as all my dreams
dance on stage,
To living a life without you, that happiness would bring.
As I dance before demons and angels the ballet of a broken
life,
And make believe that lonely sorrow hasn't been the king of
my nights.
So come dance with me my love in the thunder and the rain,
And we'll make believe we can wash away all the pain.
Dancing closer side by side,
Just make believe you'll be my husband and I'll be your
bride.
Just make believe you're my husband and I'll be with you
tonight
Beautifully dressed in purest white.
Make believe for my love.
Make believe for me please?

For I made believe for your love every day,
I made believe in every way.
That this kind of love wouldn't stay in our dreams.

Lisa
2005

THE RING

I'll let you see everything,
Just not a wedding ring.
I tied a chain around my heart,
But I gave you the part,
When I told you everything
That love could bring.
I told it all in song,
And I had to sing of everything that could bring the world to sing along.
I didn't mean to break your heart,
When we never even got a start on love like the world has ever known.
But didn't the world know just how to sing along.
They bought every line, how I wanted you for mine.
I didn't mean to make you blue,
But I couldn't stay alone, it's true.
So girl I'll show you everything,
Just not a wedding ring,
And how I tied a chain around my heart
And how you got broke apart . . .
When I told you everything that love would bring.
All the songs we'll sing about the everlasting wedding ring.
Listen to the songs of love written for the beautiful sound of a ring.
Love, won't you sing?
Love, won't you sing?
I'll show you everything,
Just not a wedding ring.
I tied a chain around your heart,
Love is love and you are art.
Now broken one, play your part.
You can have and be everything.

You hear the sounding bells of a wedding ring.
I'll show you the blues, baby are yours to sing.
I'll show you everything,
Just not a wedding ring.

Lisa
June 2007

IN A WONDERLAND

Have you ever been lonely?
Have you ever been sad?
Have you ever been left all alone with nothing to have?
What do you do with a memory so used?
What do you do with a world so confused?
Tell me how to make it on my own,
With no one to hold my hand I'm so alone?
Don't even know what it is you'd call an empty life like this.
Don't know what there is to do,
Living without love and nothing without you.
In a wonderland you could find your man
And have your toy surprise.
Through a fairy tale you'll find your husband
Looking in from the outside,
If you'll believe in lies.
Because in wonderland you were suppose to reach for the sky.
You can see it all through the tears in your eyes.
Would you hold his hand to compliment the man
With the heart of a lonely girl,
Run away to a foreign land,
Dream your dreams of a better world?
Believe he'll come today
When you see its true,
You're no longer standing in a wonderland feeling blue.
So I wonder around in a wonderland where there is no me and you.

Lisa
2005-2007

THE QUEEN BALLERINA

She's the queen-dancing ballerina.
Tell me have you seen,
Tell me have you seen her?
Princes' wears a crown,
And it isn't fallen down,
Through all her soul and heartache.
She dances all around,
She makes it with what she found,
And love cost what it takes.

She's a queen-dancing ballerina.
Tell me have you seen,
Tell me have you seen her?
Ballerina found a jukebox
And she loves the way it rocks.
The music sings to her soul.
Flies her wings heaven bound,
Soars above the ground,
Parlaying her story for the show,
One you need to know.
She's the queen ballerina.
You must have seen her dancing on the sky,
Never asking why she's got those kind of wings.
With angels she can fly and never have to cry
As her soul begins to sing.
Tell me have you seen,
Tell me have you seen,
The queen-dancing ballerina?

Lisa
1988

SOME THINGS NEVER CHANGE

I've been lost inside this empty space in my heart
And some things never change —
No . . .
How it hurts me and how it's tearing me apart,
And it just goes on and on . . .

Can you see what's on my mind?
Take a good look at my face.
Could you take the time to stand in my place?

Have you closed the door on love?
Could you be so blind?
Did you think I'd just give up?
What if I didn't want to say goodbye,
Goodbye . . .
Could you smile when inside you just want to cry?
Could you smile when it hurts so deep inside?
And it never fades away,
It never fades away . . .
It never changes on any given day,
Oh . . .

When I hear your name
Feels so cold deep inside.
Still it's hard to explain,
Oh . . .
What your love meant to me.
They say time will heal the pain,
But it never ever changed,
No . . .

It goes on forever.
And I try to find the reasons why.
I count all my mistakes
And I just cry.
How my heart aches,

Oh . . . tell me it isn't so . . . oh . . . tell me why,
We barely said hello and it was goodbye?

Can you heal my mind?
Take a look at my face.
Could you take the time to stand in my place?
No . . .
Oh . . .
Some things never change . . .

Lisa
July 9, 2007

JACKY BOY

Hey Jacky boy,
Hey Jacky boy,
You know I am your girl,
And I want to go around the world.
Hey Jacky boy,
You know I'm not a toy for you.
Hey Jacky boy,
Don't play so rough,
You'll turn me black and blue.
You take me in and out.
You leave me full of doubt.
Don't know how it's going to be,
In the game between you and me,
Jacky boy,
Jacky boy,
In the game between you and me,
Jacky boy.
You know I want to make love,
But you know I'm going to break love,
If you play me like a toy Jacky boy.
Hey Jacky boy,
Hey Jacky boy,
Come lay down beside me here on the floor,
And let me show you why you're still a boy, Jacky boy.
Come feel the fire inside of me,
I know you've been admiring me Jacky boy.
Oh Jacky boy.

Lisa
2006-2007

THE GENIUS OF THE FACADE

Not all things are what they seem to be,
And what you seem to me is the genius of the facade.
You play the prince as the proper part,
Yet you search the world as a pauper of the heart.
The musician of the fascinating charade,
But the jester of the bleeding heart parade.
Still ladies Mayfair do their best prepare
For the shining armor of the knight,
Prince Debonair, dark horse of moonlight.
Softly in the palm of his hand
He plays moonbeams over a wedding band
As every maiden ballets for the song.
He is the gentlemen of kings.
He is the ruler of thrones.
No wife would wonder beyond the voice of his song,
The sound of her king with the music to soothe her from being
alone.
Yet where is the one for whom he has played the world his stage?
Where is his love to soothe the madness of his fascinating
famous charade?
For him she wet all with wonder with the tears she cried.
His music beats the thunder of her heart inside,
As she performs passionate patience to the love she is tied.
In song he swears she must hide, Oh God,
From loves genius fascinating facade.
For no man had ever searched the earth so through,
As the performing prince, the pauper, the jester, the genius of
love so true,
Searching for love just like you.
Till this day he has found no true love,
Only the strange songs of crying doves.
They sing to him the secret of the mystery.
They say her eyes are of the moon and her words of the sea.
She tells the songs of hearts that come down from you and me.
One song you can hear clear and well
As the doves sing the song and tell . . .

Lisa

"The world is full of kings and queens
Who'll blind your eyes and steel your dreams
It's heaven and hell" (Ronnie James Dio)
"Lords are there and ladies Mayfair
who reach through your heart and steel all you care
It's heaven and hell" (me)
"_____.

_____.

It's heaven and hell" (you)
" . . . _____.

_____.

It's heaven and hell" (and you)

Lisa
2005

DARK CITY

There's no reason for living.
There's no reason that's true~.
There is no chance now dear,
I'll ever find you~.
I've been crying.
I've been crying.
And you have too~oo.
Here in this dark city,
Oh~ what can I do.
May God show his pity
On both me and you.
Because I've been trying,
I've been trying,
To find you~oo.
Yes I've been trying,
To find you~oo.
I search everywhere around me,
I walk all the avenues.
No love has ever found me,
When all I want is your arms around me,
Here in this dark city I'm midnight blue~ue.
There will be no tomorrow.
No sun can shine through,
All the empty sorrow,
I live without you~oo.
Because I've been crying.
Yes I've been crying,
And you have too.
There's no denying
Here in this dark city,
It's midnight blue~ue.
This here dark city is crying blue~ue.

Lisa

This here dark city keeps crying for you~oo.
I've been crying
And you have too~oo.

Lisa
September 11, 2007

FIR ME LAL BOOSH
(THE KISS)

Blood alive.
Alive I bleed.
My soul cries.
My soul needs.
Alive I scream.
KISS.
KISS.
KISS FREE.
Long Kiss.
Kiss me.
Alive I bleed.
Stars in my eyes,
And fir me lal boosh.
KISS.
KISS.
KISS ME.
KISS.
KISS.
KISS FREE.
My bloods alive.
My souls with thee,
In a kiss.
Fir me lal boosh.
For every day is a melody.
In every way for a fir me lal boosh.
KISS.
KISS.
KISS ME.
KISS FREE.
One,
Two,
Three,

Lisa

With a fir me lal boosh,
KISS.
KISS ME.

Lisa
December 2005

POEMS FOUND AT WWW.MYSPACE.COM

Thursday, August 19, 2010

GOD YES I LOVE YOU
Current mood: 🙂 grateful
Category: Writing and Poetry

GOD YES I LOVE YOU

Fame is like moon dust blowing in your face.
A celluloid picture that needs dusted in its place.
Moon drops on water to float you to another place.
Stars on fire burn out more dreams in space.
Time is the kiss of despair.
You and I, we're just air.

So touch me.
Please move me.
Ever so gently care.
Be that dream you wish were there.

Wishes were the willows that passed through your fingers.
Hopes were the dreams in the night we desperately needed to linger.
Our feelings set fire to the path that fame blazes.
Our madness danced across the wire of insane mazes.
A name left forever imprinted on every ones hearts, every ones faces.

Lisa

So I moved you.
Yes I touched you.
God yes I loved you.

All the songs sung that sting your soul,
There nothing like the kiss that you put to my tongue that
caused these words to know how empty I am without you,
How died out has my fire glow gasping for the warmth of the
flame that burns in you.
Love is true.
God yes I love you.

Lisa
August 18, 2010

Read more:
http://www.myspace.com/lisareneeeerickson/blog?bID=53838
8344#ixzz0x5oSEnlO

Sunday, July 11, 2010

Unrequited Love . . .
Current mood: ▨ apathetic
Category: Writing and Poetry

UNREQUITED LOVE . . .

"That there is a holiness to the heart's affection."*
In my dreams . . . lying next to a dead man's bones.
Twenty four years ago this was the life that became my own.
Here it is now, 2010, this is all I've known.
My heart use to reach for someone to hold.
A prayer to love is what I asked.
Twenty four years later a maid in waiting, I got old.
If only I could turn back time and for love not have prayed at all, for my own sake.
There is nothing from God I want to know that would cause my heart so much heart break.
Forty two years I have been alone. I have.
It doesn't matter that God came through I've always been on my own.
Many chances to love but none came through, none turned out true.
If just left with memories to only lye next to a dead man's bones
Or, the love of a good man singing on the world's stage in harmony with his most beautiful voice
Or, standing here in God's house alone.
It is the fact that in the end I'm still reaching for the wind.
Hope is the cruelest story ever told.
Even if it is true, how long should one girl lay at the bottom of the wishing well empty and cold?
I got old wishing and praying for you and only lonely poems to tell.
The prayer I asked brought me to hell.
"That there is a holiness to the heart's affection"*

Lisa

So when shall it come? This now weak and lonely heart's protection?
Some say Jehovah, and some . . . Satan's delight.
For this I must dance through the torture of the word's perfection
for the dream of love to come forth right.
Faith conceived her heart in poems.
The poetic fool of The Unrequited Dream.
The trusting soul in love's mystery.
'Oh, give me my life's breath sweet release.
For from its' beginning, love's hope . . . a simple life's dream,
by Satan's request and performed by demons—before The True God Jehovah, Christ Jesus, and Angels; Satan has asked it to be withheld from me . . . love's affection.
Mine . . . life's mirrored reflection of Love's Unrequited Dream.
'Oh, fame and glory go to hell!
With the stars whose name does care to tell?
When all life's days just passed me by
While I lay dying in the wishing well,
Filling it up with the tears I cry,
And there it is my body fell . . . found drowned in constant sorrow.
Thus again, hope shall again awaken me, resurrecting morrow.
Enticing love with the poetic words of Love's Dream . . . only to be found unrequited.

Lisa
March 4, 2010

Reference:

* Keats

Read more:
http://www.myspace.com/lisareneeerickson/
blog#ixzz0x5S7QSJ1

Sunday, July 11, 2010

UNHOLY
Current mood: 😞 rejected
Category: Writing and Poetry

UNHOLY

I walk alone, this last mile.
I look around for someone to talk to if just for a while.
Not just anyone, but someone who knows
What it means to walk the unholy road.
The one that leads to life, a promise of tomorrow.
Moments in time where there will be no more sorrow.
I walk alone . . . this unholy road,
Trying to find a world where I deserve to go.
I've searched for it all of my life.
The love of one good man who wants me to be his wife.
Together we will be a family . . . that is paradise to me.
But I still walk alone along this unholy road.
Searching for that place I must not deserve to go
Because it's been hell the whole while
I walk alone the very last mile.
Paradise for others is something they wait to see.
Yet, they got it all right there, the love of a family.
Blessed to never know what is like to be . . .
Unholy.

Lisa
July 10, 2010

Read more:
http://www.myspace.com/lisareneeerickson/
blog#ixzz0x5SG2sUW

Lisa

Monday, May 10, 2010

FIRE GOLD
Current mood: 😊 inspired
Category: Writing and Poetry

FIRE GOLD

Come in out of the rain.
My darling, yours is so much pain.
Lye here before my fire.
And I will sing you songs of desire.

Come in out from the cold.
Yes, I know, life has become so old.
But let me tell you the story of tomorrow.
It is here, lay in my arms you will find no sorrow.

I find each tear you let go.
I catch them on the wind.
I keep them in my heart,
Because I love you so my beautiful friend.

Come away from the storm.
Dry your weary eyes my love.
For the end of this life is just the beginning.
Our love in paradise will never again be separated.
Still yet to be born.
This life is not all there is.
This life is not real, it's only show biz.
I will not leave you to weather through this life alone,
I have lit the way for you to find your way home.

Come in love out from the cold.
Let my love warm your heart in fire gold.
Look forward toward all the dreams one could know.
As we watch how eternity flows.
Love, peace, and understanding they do always grow.

They come in out of the rain.
They wash away their cares, they wash away their pain.
They thrive before the fires glow.
And thus will life always go.

Lisa
May 10, 2010

Read more:
http://www.myspace.com/lisareneeerickson/
blog#ixzz0x5SeBDXw

Lisa

Sunday, April 25, 2010

Little Red Writing Hood
Current mood: 😔 stalked
Category: Writing and Poetry

LITTLE RED WRITING HOOD

As I went walking there come a wolf crossing my path, moonlight shining.., this is true.
I said, "What do you want?" He said, "Your enemies, not you."

I said, "Are you sure, you are on my path this night?"

He said, "I'm just taking it to where you won't go because you don't feel it right."

I said, "But I have forgiven my enemies. I try to forgive everyone."

He said, "I know you do, that is why justice must be done.
They have crossed your path, they have done what they have done;
And still, they never asked for forgiveness from anyone.
So, I have been sent, instinct aside, to deliver the justice for the tears you have cried.
Time has run past for the path they are on.
They must answer for the things they have done."

I said, "But what brings the moment of judgment order to decide?"

He said, "There are just so many moons, and so many tides."
Lisa

Read more:
http://www.myspace.com/lisareneeerickson/
blog#ixzz0x5Ska8M1

Thursday, April 15, 2010

Letter Of The Heart
Current mood: 🔲 lonely
Category: Writing and Poetry

LETTER OF THE HEART

Wrote a letter of the heart.
Deep inside me all the thoughts that are tearing me apart.
The tears that are standing between me and you
They have everything to do with the words locked up inside
Kept secret in the diary of my soul.
I hold the pen gently to every word I know.
In this letter of the mind,
I'm trying and trying to help you to understand.
But I can't give you the words I need you to say.
Left alone in a place in time
Writing lonely letter's of the heart and of the mind.
There's one inside just like a bird never set free.
For all that I've ever said won't bring you back to me.

Lisa
April 15, 2010

Read more:
http://www.myspace.com/lisareneeerickson/
blog#ixzz0x5SqyYV3

Lisa

Thursday, March 11, 2010

Current mood: ■ cantankerous

BLAH, BLAH, BLAH, SO WHAT, WHATEVER

SO BLAH BLAH BLAH
YEAH SO WHAT
WHATEVER
SO MANY SONGS AND POEMS
I WISH I HAD NEVER
BUT *** ** *** FOR NOW
SURE, AGAIN TOMORROW
BE ON HERE ALL DAY
SO MUCH *** *** SORROW
I KNOW YOU REALLY WANT TO HEAR IT
SO I WRITE IT ALL DOWN
BUT WHATEVER MAN
JUST ANOTHER *** POEM CLOWN
SO WHAT
WHAT OF IT
YOU THINK ITS
YOU THINK ITS WHAT
YOUT THINK ITS ***
WELL THATS EXACTLY WHY I WROTE IT DOWN
YOU INSPIRED ME YOU DIRTY, NASTY, STINKING, *** CLOWN

Missing Words:
*** ** *** = that is all
*** *** = for this
*** = foolish
*** = love
*** = thinking
Lisa March 11, 2010
Read more:
http://www.myspace.com/lisareneeerickson/
blog?page=2#ixzz0x5T2OjO7

Tuesday, January 26, 2010

BARE ABSENT MINDED
Current mood: 😑 selective
Category: Writing and Poetry

BARE ABSENT MINDED

Every once and awhile in my bare absent mind,
I get to thinking I could sure use the love in you some time.
When things go bad and I feel sick to death,
I might on occasion unconsciously whisper your name under my breath.
That's just what happens when you got nothing left.
For a slight moment I might think I'm wrong,
But soon the truth all comes back to me;
When I was with you I was bare absent minded all along.
I know you like to think that I must be lonely.
"I should have never left you," you probably say.
But the real truth is I've been worse than lonely, I'm alone,
And, when you took that drink it was you who walked away.
You knew when you walked out on me I was sick . . .
So it's been . . . sick and alone.
If your hard heartedness wasn't so thick
Your absent mindedness has struck me to the bone.
Now I know I'm so close to dying.
I thank God my tears will reach their final day.
My soul will no longer be crying . . .
It will be on its absent minded way.
But for you to know that I have foolishly loved you,
And, for a bare absent minded moment I may still just barely do.
Remember what I had told you,
You'll see it come true.
"I won't be at your funeral"
Bare absent minded love will have taken its toll.
Maybe I'll see you again,
But not if I'm smart enough to mind my soul.

Lisa

Lisa
January 26, 2010

Read more:
http://www.myspace.com/lisareneeerickson/
blog?page=4#ixzz0x5TQGV9m

Thursday, January 07, 2010

Remember This One Thing
Category: Writing and Poetry

REMEMBER THIS ONE THING

Always to remember this one thing.
It's not easy for the guilty or the victim.
Always having to swim in the river of sin.
I think if I were in their shoes I would need and want to be forgiven.
So I have forgiven and all of us just go on living.
But I wish that they would do one thing for me.
Don't make forgiveness the second crime to make you even more guilty.
So I may need to tell my story but you think I just won't let go so how could I have really forgiven?
If you truly valued forgiveness you would deal with the consequences that others may know and you too just try to keep on living.
We both get to live with this horrible thing but what value would you make of Christ if you do not accept the forgiveness and the consequences your actions bring?
Just because I have trouble always remembering this one thing?
To be forgiven is needed by both great and small.
But to forgive ourselves is the hardest of all.
Always to remember this one thing?

Lisa
January 07, 2010

Read more: http://www.myspace.com/lisareneeerickson/
blog?page=4#ixzz0x5TWkZQR

Lisa

Saturday, December 26, 2009

HEART BROKEN TRAIN
Current mood: 😊 mellow
Category: Writing and Poetry

HEART BROKEN TRAIN

'B' said he was leaving,
He's going to hop a train.
I said, "I won't hold you up babe,
But please remember me should I never see you again."
Here today.
Gone tomorrow.
Neither here nor there
Yet, still a little farther than anything I ever felt before.

'B' got down to the tracks
And heard the whistle in the air.
Put his ear down to the rail
To see if he could hear his heart beat there.
Here today.
Gone tomorrow.
Neither here nor there
Yet, still a little farther than anything I ever felt before.

The track's shook and the train rolled right along.
'B' pulled out his Harmony and began to play his song.
Long, long whistle blow
Sweetest sound he'd ever know.

(Harmonica solo)

Here today.
Gone tomorrow.
Neither here nor there
Yet, still a little farther than anything I ever felt before.

Down about 3 miles or so
Lights were flashing and the crossing bars came down low.
Trucks came to a stop, wouldn't dare go further don't you know.
Here today.
Gone tomorrow.
Neither here nor there
Yet, still a little farther than anything I ever felt before.

'B' sat watching with guitar in hand.
Felt the rhythm of the train rolling.
Heard those chords way down in his soul.
Moved all the strings of his heart he'd ever know.

(Guitar solo)

Here today.
Gone tomorrow.
Neither here nor there
Yet, still a little farther than anything I ever felt before.

'B' waited patiently with his song in his heart.
The train just stopped 500 ft. before him and wouldn't part.
'B' still felt that time would tell,
He'd wait and hop that car, he just as well.
Here today.
Gone tomorrow.
Neither here nor there
Yet, still a little farther than anything I ever felt before.

'B' sat all day as the sun set and the moon began to laugh at him.
The train never budged or blew steam again.
Train conductor stepped down, sat down, sang awhile and drank some beer.
He said, " 'B' why are you here today?
You'll be gone tomorrow.
You'll be neither here nor there

Yet, still a little farther than anything you've ever felt before."

'B' just laughed but with a tear in his eyes
Said, "My baby wouldn't stop me so I said goodbye.
Here today.
Gone tomorrow.
Neither here nor there,
Yet, still a little farther than anything I should have ever had to feel before."

Lisa

In memory of Mike Brown. "B" December 25, 1959 - February 7, 1992:

Read more:
http://www.myspace.com/lisareneeerickson/
blog?page=5#ixzz0x5TrWwoB

Monday, November 30, 2009

Recipe: Babylon Bread
Current mood: ☺ contemplative
Category: Writing and Poetry

(THE GREAT) BABYLON BREAD
'Made by Harlot's Everywhere'
"Men serve this dish cold." REQUIRED!

Ingredients:

Lot's of Pagan Holiday Spice.
1 cup Shintoism.
4 Buddhist Noble Truths.
1 Yin.
1 Yang.
1 Handful of Confucianism.
1 Mahayana Buddhist Doctrine of the Word.
1 Slice of Taoism.
1 Chunk of Baptist; 1st, 2nd, or 3rd.
1 Heaping TBLS. of Baal Idol Worship.
1/4 Cup of 1st Christian; sifted down into 2nd and 3rds.
1 Whole, Devout Lutheran, Uncompromised.
1 Peace of Paradise in Heaven Instead of on Earth.
1/8 TSP. of Amish or Mennonite Way.
1 or 2 Proverbs of Jim Jones or David Koresh, chilled, let set out to fester after that.
Ice Each Ingredient with Motsuri goto (things pertaining to idol worship).

Note: When shopping for these ingredients, look for The Way. If you can't find it then it would be better to take the cramped road because the wide road has a lot of traffic. Apply to the God of Good Luck for the money to support the above listed ingredients. Follow allegiance to any National Flag along the way with a full blown heart of a terrorist so no one will get in the way of your mission, and, pray to the God of War for power to make this entrusted mission, of which only you could fulfill, to reach its Kamikaze stage.

After you have baked all of the half-baked ingredients, mix everything using a phallic symbol in The Holy Trinity Bowl then pour mixture into the Heavenly Donation Arrangement Plate from The House of Zion, bake in hellfire and damnation of Catholicism for an eternity; or, at this point you could leave it to sit in Purgatory forever at a cost of such that is eternally undecided (Someone else will know for how long and for how much, at least you'd think so but no one knows who). Also, do not forget to Tithe as well at this point. This will all work out best if you continually Tithe. Continually. Continually. Always Tithe. I can't stress the importance of this enough. It is adamant that you TITHE! I said TITHE DAMN YOU!!! (Oh, please excuse me, it gets hot in this kitchen) If this is too hard you can always try the 7th Day Adventist approach, or, you could just do it Yahweh, if not, you could always sit around and hope for a Heavenly reward in the Promise Land (also now known as The City of Refuge) for the Jews. Be careful though because things can get real ugly there.

While cooking you may begin to recognize 'the sound of one hand clapping (Koans)' but this is normal. Remain apathetic until you see 'the writing on the wall' or the flood has come and gone. You may try to build up to a Nirvana in order to find that all really is in a truly pure and good state, but don't, just be sure and chant "Aummm" every once and awhile to make sure all is one. Magic, Soothsaying, and Incantations will not help you at this point. You could call 1134 (hEll) for to speak to Elijah but even he couldn't tell you what you could expect at this point. It will bake best at high altitudes such as a Monastery or a Nunnery. A little pinch of hashish, gaunga, or illicit drugs at this point couldn't hurt. Cover with a National Flag of your choice until hard and loyal. Be a true believer and have some sort of faith for a time, times, and half a time that all of this really and truly does lead everyone to the same place (Most people will tell you that it does all lead to the same place).

And, on that note: whilst preparing and serving things, things have changed in "The Kitchen". Women are able to take the lead. This dish can prepare men for salvation although it tends to prepare women for reincarnation as men. This recipe can also turn men into women who can now take the lead (Finally!) in 'Hell's Kitchen'. Now see if you can get out of hellfire with what you've done. Watch it! It's hot. To help cool things down for you a bit begin to add 1 ounce of philosophy teachings from any of 'The Great Philosophers' that there are. You can even ask your neighbor if he has some, your choice, or you don't even have to decide because does it really matter? Think about it. Then add at least 1 ounce, at your discretion, from your own philosophies. You're The Greatest Philosopher Ever! Let rise on the 3rd day in an Easter Basket.

Do not forget to break this bread and pass it around to everyone and I MEAN EVERYBODY. Don't just choose 144,000 of Jesus closest Jewish friends. That was the first party; they were selfish with the bread. Jesus said this is a new party and everyone's invited! Good News! Every egg of every color and you're to go out by two's, at the least, to find them so you can include them in the party. Now you should also have some wine, pass the bottle around. "Eat, drink; be merry, for tomorrow ye shall die!" Now while eating you may experience signs in heaven and strange phenomenon but relax, chill baby, it's a party. That's just the impending destruction coming upon all wicked mankind for eating this type of bread and for those who spread it around as if they were doing many fine works in sight of the Lord. That is why you will hear a strange voice from Heaven say; "Get away from me you workers of lawlessness, I know you not." Just don't sweat from the yoke of these labors. Just "Eat, drink, and be merry for tomorrow ye shall die!" Be defiant and independent! You can mix these ingredients in any manner you choose because they all lead to the same place; you can even bake your own bread and sell it commercially.

However, if you find this type of food to be tasteless and disgusting and you hear the growling sound of a huge chasm of spiritual emptiness in your belly and what you have been feeding yourself on has suddenly become completely undesirable then I would suggest you throw it out, walk away from it, and call on The Great Physicians', The Great Healers' Jehovah and Jesus. This is a Father, Son doctor team. They can help you to see that when you went to sit and chow down at a table you got stumbled and sat down at the wrong table, even though there are really only two tables to have chosen from. The table belonging to Satan and his Demons who feed people disgusting, fowl, rotten, nasty, bread. And, there is the table that belongs to Jehovah, Jesus, and the Angels.

So fear not, this does not have to be your last supper if you don't choose to make it so. To receive a more joyful and satisfying meal, seek meatier understanding of the scriptures from which will come 'The Bread Of Life'. You will sit at the table of majestic dignity, uncompromisable nobility of character and peace, with a joyful mind and plenty of nourishing, life sustaining, spiritual food and good conversation. You will never feel sick or hungry for truth again. You can even live forever and never die from eating and enjoying a meal with The One True God and his son, Jesus Christ. You just follow this recipe for "The Bread Of Life."

"THE BREAD OF LIFE"

Thumb every page of 'The Good Book' cook book.
Season with a pinch of right understanding.
A dash of right mindedness.
More than a smidgeon of good speech to bubble forth.
Several pecks of right action.
A gallon a day of right living.
A measure of good effort.
A tinge of sincere attentiveness.
A fair amount of complete meditation and concentration.

Add these ingredients with a regular quart of bible study with one of Jehovah's Witnesses. Then you must pound and knead this life giving bread until it ferments your whole heart, your whole soul, and your whole mind. Do this with your whole strength but remember to bake with 'the power beyond what is normal out of God and not that out of yourself'. Let yourself, rest in Jehovah and see all those who will partake of this Heavenly Bread on a Paradise Earth. Store this bread up within yourself and do not let it go stale and Jehovah will make it grow in you to feed the many if you will share generously with others.

Once you have received the true "Bread Of Life" still always pray, 'give us this day our daily bread' and give thanks to Jehovah, in Jesus name. Amen. Call on Jehovah's name because if you don't and you are just saying "GOD" you could be talking to any one of those false GODS created by Satan and he's just going to feed you some real nasty molded Babylon bread.

Lisa
9/2008-11/30/2009

Reference:

Moore-Bruder Philosophy
The Power of Ideas, 6th Edition, Chapt. 15, p. 522
'Eastern Influence'

The New World Translation of The Holy Scriptures

Read more:
http://www.myspace.com/lisareneeeerickson/
blog?page=5#ixzz0x5TzvTXi

Lisa

Friday, November 13, 2009

"Freedom, Beauty, Truth, Love"*
Current mood: ▨ accomplished
Category: Writing and Poetry

"FREEDOM, BEAUTY, TRUTH, LOVE"*

And so we have sung our secret song.
We have whispered 'our' nothing's wrong.
And though the night be always long
To stare into Hade could be no wrong.
With blood drained eyes of love
Our tears have dripped down into the deep wells of Hell.
Today is tomorrow and yesterday
And love lay bleeding because our life is love's tale . . .
The show must go on
Thunders the sound of the funeral drum.
Sacrifice your heart with mine as one
And let it be sung the purest of love's mystery hum . . .
Love escapes death.
Love is life's breath.
"There is no greater thing to ever learn than to love and be loved in return"*
But to live to love again.
Too dance side by side over earth above.
Too sing 'our' secret song of love
With the purest voice 'nothing's wrong.'

It's all right now;
Love Lisa.
11-11-09

Reference:
*Moulin Rouge
Read more:
http://www.myspace.com/lisareneeerickson/
blog?page=5#ixzz0x5U7KHG4

Friday, October 02, 2009

THE SONGS OF THE SIRENS
Current mood: 😔 breezy

Category: Writing and Poetry

Where the "Songs of the Sirens" are sung don't you know,
It is there where we are to go . . . mad in ecstasy . . . you and me.
Traveling to a place where man does not return from, nor wants too.
More than paradise or more than we deserve it's true
But I am there in your arms with you . . . forever listening to the most beautiful sound I ever could hear . . . your love. I'd die there and still live forever . . . in that place where the "Songs of the Sirens" are heard.

Lisa

Oct. 2, 2009

Read more:
http://www.myspace.com/lisareneeerickson/
blog?page=5#ixzz0x5UFMAnH

Lisa

Wednesday, July 22, 2009

"THE LEVEE"

Current mood: 🫤 miserable
Category: Writing and Poetry

THE LEVEE

Walking so long now down by the levee
I'm living so long now here in Misery (Missouri)
Can't get the things Lord I so dearly need
Wonder what will happen to poor ol' me

Shouldn't there be the light of day Lord that I would see
My shoes have worn out walking this levee
Just might fall in and let the river take me
Don't know if I'm to sink or swim or float out to sea
All I know is Misery wants to swallow me

Lisa
July 11, 2009

Read more: http://www.myspace.com/lisareneeerickson/
blog?page=6#ixzz0x5UZg2VK

Sunday, July 05, 2009

DREAMS
Current mood: 🙁 discontent
Category: Writing and Poetry

DREAMS

Starring out to reach for something that will never be
Through the prison of my mind where he holds me.
Useless are the tears that try to flee.
He tortures each one and never sets them free.
Since visitors are none for what have you come to see?
The talent,
The rhyme,
The heart's rhythm,
The mime,
The clown,
The moon,
The words?
Nothing was said that love heard . . .
Wha . . . ?
Dreaming is useless to break free,
My spirit is dead inside of me.
In my mirror my reflection has left me.
Nothing mortal could I ever be.
So tell me are you happy?
My tears fall like rain and slide down glisteningly the bars of
my room.
I stare out and call for help from the moon
And from the dark side he stares back and reflects to me
that this is my tomb.

Lisa
June 24, 2009
Read more:
http://www.myspace.com/lisareneeerickson/
blog?page=6#ixzz0x5UipNIO

Lisa

Wednesday, June 24, 2009

Jun 24, 2009

NOW

Current mood: 😊 amused
Now . . .
What I never wrote the night before is probably more true than what I'll ever write today.
Now, Nah, Never, Nope, Not if, NO, Not, Nuh uh, Nay, Nothing, now . . .
If you believe me then I would say have it your way . . .
"Whatever you want babe, whatever you need, just as long as you know babe"*
that what I never wrote in the line before is probably more true than what I will write in the next one.
I hate your guts my god you make me sick.
Now.
Now you're beautiful. But whatever I could write next has got to be more of a lie than what I just wrote. Are you with me on this?
Where am I at?
What am I doing?
When was this I supposedly did it?
Why would I even do such a thing?
How could you accuse me of such a lie?
What I am telling you at this moment, now, right now, is the God's honest truth so you better listen to what I am about to say . . . now, nah, never, nope, not if, no, not, nuh uh, nay, nothing, now . . . I just have no excuse for being in love with you when you obviously couldn't believe a word I say.
What ever I could say NOW, it will wait till you think it is the right time if you just want me to keep it to myself,
Now?_____ . . .

Reference: Nazareth

Lisa
06/24/2009

190

Friday, June 12, 2009

HEART OF FIRE
Current mood: ■ confident
Category: Writing and Poetry

HEART OF FIRE

The Devil plays with thee . . . you and me.
Time there comes to make your stand,
Hold me though you have not the hand.
Heart of fire comes not from hell,
But burns the lies that other's tell.
Eyes of understanding are what I see
But the Devil keeps them hidden from me.
Still, the sound of honesty rings true
And I clearly have seen and heard you.
The Devil's time is so short.
The harder and faster he'll come at this report.
Touch honesty.
Feel truth.
Speak genuine.
Follow not the rest of men.
Heart of fire comes not from hell,
But burns the lies that other's tell.
Heart of fire will heal me and bring me back, faith, you'll see.
Jehovah and a heart of fire are all I need.
When I looked in your eyes I was not afraid to bleed.

Lisa
06/11/09

Read more:
http://www.myspace.com/lisareneeerickson/
blog?page=6#ixzz0x5V5c69i

WHA . . . . ?

Peace, love, and happiness has left her building a homeless heart,
There the trees have hid her and the ground did bid her
"Nay, never walk the earth again, search as you may for here you'll find no friend."
For crying not lightly you must go your way.
Into the night sleep flee from what lies love would say.
Maddened mercy shall fend for you Dearest Saddened Lady.
So let the men of the earth for you go crazy,
"Bid her answer her door once more!"
Yeah though never shall it be . . .
Less one question answered unto thee . . .
"Wha . . . . ?"

Lisa
05/27/09

My treasure house was made of words.
Knocking, knocking, knocking,
I heard.
I opened to hear all the answers but it was all the questions that were disturbed.

Read more:
http://www.myspace.com/lisareneeerickson/
blog?page=7#ixzz0x5VC88CV

Saturday, May 09, 2009

Mystical
Current mood: lonely
Category: Writing and Poetry

MYSTICAL

My love . . . he is so mystical.

He is beyond the stars.

I reach for him but he is too high for me.

I cannot have him but I want him.

I cannot be with him but I need him.

I cannot hold him but I love him.

It is his universe.

I wish I were.

My love . . . he is so mystical.

The trees hush the wind not to blow,

But to carry the sound of the voice of his song just so.

The moon whispers his name.

The sun announces him just the same.

The stars fade out before his fame.

Gladly they all play in his choir.

The songs sung move the earth

And all its children dance around the fire.

Were I to be one time and space,

I would cling to the moment we see each other's face.

Time would stand still and all of the world would know . . .

My love . . . he is mystical.

Lisa
May 9, 2009

Read more:
http://www.myspace.com/lisareneeerickson/
blog?page=7#ixzz0x5VJC2FD

Saturday, March 21, 2009

MIRROR, MIRROR
Current mood: 🁣 exanimate
Category: Writing and Poetry

MIRROR, MIRROR

Through the mirror I've turned to look over my shoulder at all the reasons for all the changes I've ever made.
I have found the reasons for all the changes are behind me now so to the mirror before me the future will be laid . . . its price rock hard to be paid.
But when I still can see the cost my love has paid for all the reasons (persons) that won't and don't walk with me to the future of which I am lead—ALONE.
I have found to look in a mirror now for a glimmer of hope just to see those who wanted left behind tells me I was love blind for hearts of stone.
If I could just take one of those cold hearted stones to break this mirror before me I must face everyday then maybe I won't be looking through this mirror over my shoulder for a future that never cared to be there for me anyway.
When I look in the mirror I look for you, not for me . . . see this is what I see. Are you past, present or future for me?
What do you see?

Lisa
March 21, 2009

Read more:
http://www.myspace.com/lisareneeerickson/
blog?page=7#ixzz0x5VOojGQ

Sunday, January 18, 2009

STARS OF SWEET BELIEF
Current mood: 😊 impervious
Category: Writing and Poetry

STARS OF SWEET BELIEF

1st verse:
Lie to me. C'mon and lie to me. Tell me that you love me. Tell me that I'm everything you'll ever need. Go on baby, and lie to me.

2nd verse:
So c'mon and make me see everything you wish I'd believe. Wrap me up in your fantasy. C'mon baby, lie to me.

3rd verse:
In the nights that we sleep alone I know you're out there on your own. I'll comfort you in a night of dreams and make you feel that love is what it seems. All your dreams they have come true. I'll make believe in this lie for you.

(Repeat 1st verse)
Lie to me. C'mon and lie to me. Tell me that you love me. Tell me that I'm everything you'll ever need. Go on baby and lie to me.

4th verse:
Maybe this love is smoke and mirrors and all I'll ever have are my own tears. Still I know if that were true the most beautiful lie I ever believed, I believed in you.

5th verse:
And so my love let's make sweet belief; for if but nothing, you've given my lonely heart relief and held my hand through life, you've kept me; because The Truth of The Lie is what I need.

(Repeat 1st verse)
So c'mon baby and lie to me. C'mon and lie to me. Tell me that you love me. Tell me that I'm everything you'll ever need. Go on baby and lie to me. I promise to make sweet belief for the truth of the lie in love, such sweet relief, my sweet belief. My sweet belief. C'mon and lie to me.

Lisa
11/18/2009

Read more:
http://www.myspace.com/lisareneeerickson/blog?page=7#ixzz0x5VTWcjr

Sunday, November 09, 2008

SO SAD TO BE LONELY

Current mood: 🔲 lonely
Category: Writing and Poetry

When the shadow turns upon my face if you really loved me you would find the trace of constant sorrow as I search for just a little of you before my eyes. You would see that they cry and cry and never dry because joy might have smiled upon me today. You would come to change how this must be this way and you would stay to make me smile. Make me smile. When shadow covers my day I pray that somehow I could know you won't leave me alone this way. But years have come and gone and every day my eyes have pleaded on and on for a moment of love. What is love? Why is what love is not looking for me? Why are lonely shadows all that hold me? Why won't love come to know me? So sad to be lonely.

(I wrote the paragraph poem but the title belongs to a song by Janis Joplin)
Lisa
11/09/2008

Read more:
http://www.myspace.com/lisareneeerickson/
blog?page=7#ixzz0x5VsCIZF

Thursday, September 25, 2008

CAGES BY DESIGN

Current mood: ▨ crushed
Category: Writing and Poetry

Cages by design
Closed and locked
Over heart and mind.
The seagull of her heart she's encaged.
She hold's herself so hard now
Her own love is dying madly estranged.
She holds herself so hard so now she will not breathe.
She's caged by design and she alive in love will never leave.
Love squeezed
Death's door released.
This cage by design.
The one free seagull who sweetly sang over her heart and her mind with rhythms so sweet and so kind
Has wrapped her own arms up around her as he has never found her . . . Free,
But only to die in her heart caged by design.
A singing songbird of the sea caged by design, were never Free.
But every part of her so wanted to be.

Lisa
September, 20, 2010

Read more:
http://www.myspace.com/lisareneeerickson/
blog?page=7#ixzz0x5Vxb6KX

Lisa

Wednesday, September 24, 2008

TO LOVE A STAR
Current mood: ■ awake
Category: Writing and Poetry

TO LOVE A STAR

It is the time
The midnight star shine,
To lay herself down in your heart . . . to cry herself to sleep at
night. He would sing "I promise if you hold with me you will be
all right".
It is the time
He'd hold her tight and dry her tears.
He's loved her through all these years.
He leads himself through the galaxy but she cannot keep up
till the morning to see what he sees.
She hurts so bad . . . not just from her heart but the physical
pain trying to remain the only one he really needs. She
bleeds . . .
She asks herself . . .
Will I wake, will I rise, will I live, will I cry,
Is it the time the midnight star die?
It is the time
He should know why she cries . . .
the only way his midnight star will ever shine is when she is
kept in his eyes.

Lisa

09/24/2008

Read more:
http://www.myspace.com/lisareneeerickson/
blog?page=7#ixzz0x5W4BJvL

THE QUEENS GEMS

Current mood: ▦ forgotten
Category: Writing and Poetry

THE QUEENS GEMS

The most brilliant dazzling gems belonging to the queen do sparkle so softly before her gentle eyes.
Each jewel came parading down before her to be viewed by one and all, every fair maiden and courting gent at the lonely loons midnight ball.
So softly they sparkled as if they held some mystery of love gone mad, times that had passed into the oceans lonely sea.
Still fair maidens and duchesses alike, socialites and aristocrats sat conniving on how they might just posses one for their own hidden treasures held secret in name. To take from the Queen was only fair game.
No brave night came as the defender of such jewels, especially of the blue diamond heart for fear it was at best cruel. The queen wondered around the halls and dungeons lonely of the nights. She carried her jewels constantly and they glowed in the moonlight. One by one they sparkled and would shine in her hair. They fell everywhere so daintily across the form of her body as nothing else was there. No warmer touch, nor tender caress, no words of love or her heart to be blessed she had ever heard or felt. She prayed unceasingly for the mercy of love soon but there was no sound to return to her at the midnight ball of the lonely loon. So. she playfully caught them one by one surprisingly within her hands and wondered what afraid of these were man, the most rarest treasure ever of earth, but no one felt what her tears were worth..

Lisa
June 25, 2008

Read more:
http://www.myspace.com/lisareneeerickson/
blog?page=8#ixzz0x5WY8aOe

Lisa

Thursday, June 12, 2008

THE ETHEREAL UNIVERSE
Current mood: 😞 bummed
Category: Writing and Poetry

THE ETHEREAL UNIVERSE

Here in the ethereal madness of my mind
I try to escape what I always seem to find.
But still held captive to an insane degree
I may never be with you and you may never be with me.
Hope grows in my heart like a cancerous disease
Just so I can believe in what may never really be.
And hope can watch me fall to my knees
To see me begging 'please' for just a moment in time . . . you with me.
All my thoughts are just stars in space.
I go from one to other to try and find a place
In the ethereal madness held to an insane degree.
Out here without you is not what I want to be
In this prison made vast just for me . . . The Ethereal Universe.

Lisa

June 12, 2008
Read more
http://www.myspace.com/lisareneeerickson/
blog?page=8#ixzz0x5WcMxe2

Tuesday, May 06, 2008

Hello, You've Reached The Moon. What Would You Like To Say To The Man In The Moon?
Current mood: 😊 virginal
Category: Writing and Poetry

HELLO, YOU'VE REACHED THE MOON, WHAT WOULD YOU LIKE TO SAY TO THE MAN IN THE MOON? (homeless in Clinton Mo, long ago)

When I called you . . .
My heart was on the line.
And when I first saw you . . .
So became my mind.
It wasn't until seven years ago I first seen your face,
Even though it was more than fifteen years ago our phone conversation could ever be traced.
But if you followed the tides of the pattern of the moon,
Every moment has bled as deep as the ocean away to your room where I could open the doors to your sweet sleep of the night, and feel your loving arms holding me tight.
Your eyes take me away to the only place I ever want to be . . .
In the arms of the man who will one day see, hear, and love me.
So when I call to you my heart is on the line.
And when you see me know that though it had begun it is still the beginning of time.
And as the moon circles round the ocean's way, the sun hears the sound of moment's who'll say . . .
Past, present, and future trace forever the tears of this love through time, and no matter when you'll always be mine. I love you.

Lisa
May 06, 2008

Read more: http://www.myspace.com/lisareneeerickson/blog?page=8#ixzz0x5WieWvN

MUSIC IS LOVELY

So nice to see people remain friends.
Music is lovely.
No matter what color
You'll always be a friend to me.
Music is so lovely.
Can reach the heart of every woman, every man.
No walls to overcome.
No front line military stand.
Music just slips through the open door
Where the heart can't fight anymore.
Takes a soul by the hand;
Does all it can, it'll lift you back up,
It will be a friend.
Music is lovely.
Music is lovely.
It makes a sweet song of you and me.
Yes . . . music is lovely.
Music can heal a broken heart,
Take life back to the start.
Fly the soul toward the future,
Clear away the storms of nature,
Break apart man's hatred.
Music can make the romance,
It brings together for the dance,
It marks the times of our lives.
It sooths the mind broken inside.
It tells the stories of mankind
And keeps our history close to mind.
Music is so lovely.
So lovely,
Music is lovely,
So, so lovely,
Music.

Lisa
July 2010

Inspired by the story of the lifetime career of The Greg Allman Band.

It is a song and carries a sound like that of The Greg Allman Bands song "Please Call Home."

Lisa

TIME IS RELATIVE

Time moves backwards . . . so fast, so very fast. You have present creating future. Light and Dark create matter. They fight for space. They charge. Thus charge matter into life, into light. Light is more powerful than dark. Dark is the foundation in which light stands on. Moving forward from moving back from where dark had been. Dark loses its place as it finds another. It is after all . . . only dark. What is there when light is not? Empty dark. Light is the neurotransmitter emanating from Jehovah's finger. When issued forth it moves backward over dark spaces. Dark flees creating another space, then present appears to begin future. Dark is Jehovah's paper to write on, his canvas to paint on. Light is in all Jehovah's creation, even in darkness if he wants it there. Don't think so? Just watch the snow channel as dark and light, light and dark compete for space. That is just man's channel. Remember you are on God's channel.

Lisa 2005

Sep 18, 2010

ALL THAT I AM, ALL THAT I CHOOSE, I DID ALREADY LOSE.

Current mood:☺depressed

My voice sings love for you on the air
In my life that's all that's there.
I hear yours sing and I know you love me, that you care
The only way our lips will ever kiss
Beautiful, but it isn't fair
To love the unavailable man is the ultimate sin
But when I began to love you that is not what you were then
To stop loving you is to take in the ultimate death of soul again
Your voice haunts me
Your beautiful form taunts me
And madness has become my only lover
And madness offers nothing to cover the bitterness of my soul
I stand alone on the stage of life in a twisted role before demons and angels
Boxed seats set aside especially for Jehovah, Jesus, and Satan
The words I speak are unplanned, my own freewill
Will I keep integrity or will I let my blood spill
Standing before heaven and hell facing the world's final curtain call
Everybody thinks they know when they know nothing at all
And nobody knows baby
Nobody knows this lady
The choice between everlasting life and everlasting glory and fame
They believe riches are the only choice in this game
Tell me you wouldn't be confused by it all, where to make your name
When your soul is full of rock-n-roll

Lisa

Your heart holds out a river of blues
And the soul is in desperate need of the love in you
And common sense tells you this wicked world will have to
come to their end
And then to just turn around night after night in an empty bed
while madness caresses your head, knowing the whole while
all you really want is to be touched by the one you love way
down inside.
So I have cried and cried, prayed to have died, woke up to live
the fine line between heaven and hell, and never can tell if you
really understand.
All that I am, all that I choose, I did already lose.

Lisa
09/16/2010

Oct 20, 2010
Poet And The Peep
Current mood:😊impervious

POET AND THE PEEP

This city, this sea of people.
This strange dream but all so real.
These great wonderlands of both holy and unholy man,
Only stand righteous and unrighteous by those who say they
can.

And don't they! Don't they! Don't they all! Yeah Youooooo!

So with the crowds shadow cast in heavy shroud
Bear down on me and lift me up above the ground
To stand and turn to them all
To sing to them the sad song of man's fall,
Icarus!
Icarus!
Icarus!
And don't they! Don't they! Don't they all! Youoooooooo—!

Singing songs of the siren.
The musical madness of the Poet and the Peep
Drowning, in the saddest of river's deep.
In her blood; through her veins; the mad, mad world can weep.
Dream . . . evermore in peaceful sleep.
And don't they!! Don't they!! Don't they all!!!! All Youoooooooo
oooooooooooo!!!!!!!!!!!!!!!!!!!!!

Lisa 10/18/2010

Dec 13, 2010

MY DEEPEST LOVE

I'll create the world of your dreams.
You'll tell me what it seems.
You tell me what you want in it.
I'll tell you what it means.
(Wind Chimes Ring)
You want that world around you.
So hope all your dreams have found you.
But baby can you tell what is real?
Tell me what you feel.

Are those clouds on the horizon
Where all your hopes are lying
Or does rain fill the air
And leave you wondering where you'll find me?

It's in the vault of your dreams.
It's in the cave.
It's in the deep
Where you're enslaved.
It's in the ground.
It's in the air.
It's in your heart.
It's everywhere.
Eternity is always there
And you will run to me.
Yes you will come to see
My deepest love.

Lisa
December 08, 2010

Dec 18, 2010

In Love's Crescendo

IN LOVE'S CRESCENDO

Two hearts dating in measured time,
Through every song,
Every word,
Every rhyme,
Because I know the heart of you,
You are mine.

Two hearts in love measure time.
Singing songs of sweet release,
Love making crying.
The music of two souls intertwined,
Because you know the heart of me,
I am yours in like, I am yours in kind.

Measure you,
Measure me.
One heart measures time.
Love is love each second,
Each hour,
Each day we find ourselves
For eternity
In the groove,
So smooth,
In love's matched crescendo .

Lisa
December 16, 2010

Tuesday, May 06, 2008

THE BATTLE OF EVERMORE

What were I to do with love
That love has not all ready done to me?
Were I to play the game
Love would never let me be.
Come one lover,
Come two lover,
Come three lover,
Come four.
Yes I know that I can love any man
As long as I'll agree to love him more.
The source of love is the what for.
You can never love me enough
If I'm not handing it to you for sure.
Work your ways
And live your days
As if you never knew what for.
But here comes one lover,
Comes two lover,
Comes three lovers,
And always another for sure.
What bed would I make for love in order to please?
For I all ready know too many times that love would break me
to my knees.
I no longer pray for love
Nor want to find you at my door.
I done gave you all my love
Now tell me why would you want more?
Come one lover,
Come two lover,
Come three lover,

And yes, you will have more.
But know no love,
No love
Like my love evermore.

Lisa
January 1, 2011

PARADISE GARDEN

Baby, baby let me love you with all that I have.
Baby, baby I need you so bad.
My sweet darling come hold me.
Tell me you love me and never set me free.
Come here now love be by my side.
Touch me with your love deep inside.
Put your arms around me and feel me tremble this way.
Let your love surround me it's going to please me all my days.
The future is now love we can no longer wait.
So come now my sweet dear don't you hesitate.
We'll dream for tomorrow but we live for today.
Happiness and true love is our good loving way.
Paradise is sweet and I'll meet you in the garden my babe.

Chorus:
Put in a garden, a place for two.
In the paradise garden I'm going to need you.
So we see and we can feel.
In your arms paradise is real.

Lisa
January 10, 2011

THANK YOU JEHOVAH

Butterflies in sunrise,
Dragonflies in moon skies,
Light that breaks through the window at the close of a summer
afternoon.
Every single flower found before, after, and during the month
of June.
Friends who don't find a need to cry.
The day that last forever where all the righteous live and never
die.
The sacrifice of Jesus for all the sin in I.
The creations of Jehovah meant to be enjoyed.
Gift of family given never to be destroyed.
Little children's kisses,
Human wishes,
Tasty dishes,
The place in time allowed to know you.
Thank you Jehovah.

Lisa

The Revelation To Come
Current mood: 😊 inspired
Category: Writing and Poetry

THE REVELATION TO COME

Above the stars, before the moon, on a sunny day comes love so soon.
Where time leaves few traces but memory replaces the lines on your face.
Your soulful eyes show tears you have cried of the dreams unseen.
A window opened deep into your soul hid forever in your dreams . . .
I am the love you know; I am your gentle Queen.
Peace, love, and harmony are all that we need, all that's between you and me.
All other roads lead to madness and I shall find no other gladness than to be your dancing slave girl.
I will be happy to do all that you bid, and be the most blessed to have your kids, and see you as King of my world.
So time will leave no traces of bad memories that place lines on my face.
My soulful eyes shall never show tears I will have cried of dreams unseen.
Through an open window into my soul, my love you shall go, my gentle King.
You're all that I need, peace, love, and harmony is always between you and me.
Above the stars and before the moon on a sunny day come love so soon.

Written today, May 6th, 2008, for a secret love I have kept very long in my heart. The Revelation To Come.

Lisa.
Read more:

http://www.myspace.com/lisareneeerickson/
blog?page=8#ixzz0x5Wqb0pc

Saturday, April 12, 2008

THE PRAYER

Current mood: 😌 blessed
Category: Writing and Poetry

Dear Jehovah,

Somewhere *in my world,*
Is this man *in my dreams,*
His eyes *are of understanding,*
His smile *of appreciation.*
Hands *so gentle,*
And body *so sweet.*
Trust in me.
Faith in me.
Love for me.
This man in my dreams,
Will he stay *in my dreams*?

In Jesus name I pray, Amen. Lisa 1985♥

First read The Prayer Poem, then read the words in Times New Roman only, and then read only the words in calligraphy.

This is a prayer I prayed to Jehovah God after learning his name from the bible when I was 18 years old. I learned this from Jehovah's Witnesses. I also learned I could ask for anything in Jesus name according to Jehovah's will, believe that I have received it and it will be mine. So I wanted to serve God and I wanted real love, good love, from a very good man. That is what I prayed for. When I wrote it I had too many commas in each line and nothing to do that day because of strange and weird occurrence, so I went back and rewrote each line in a

Lisa

different color except for the heading and the closing, because they did not have too many commas. When I read the words down written in black, this was my fears of what I prayed for, of being used by a man. I'm sure we are all afraid of getting used by someone we might love. When I went back and read the words written in red it told me my answer to what I had prayed for. It was scary and I tried to hide but there was no where I could hide. It took me 15 years but now I don't hide it anymore, I am one of Jehovah's Witnesses now and I declare his name to everyone. As for finding that love I prayed for, not yet, but when it is Jehovah God's will, I will find him then.

Read more:
http://www.myspace.com/lisareneeerickson/
blog?page=8#ixzz0x5WvgxNC

218

ABOUT THE AUTHOR

P oetry for those who have or haven't found love. Poetry for anyone who never had the love they gave be equal in return.

I was born in Marshall Missouri on July 8, 1967. I had written the poem 'The Prayer' when I was 18 years old. Before that there are only a couple of poems I had written in high school that were published in the local paper and plastered on Grandma and Grandpa Howery's refrigerator (my proudest moments). These are the only writing qualifications I had.

I attended Marshall High School and my greatest influence to work a writing career was my English teacher, Authorene Phillips. After Marshall High School ' I won 1988 Honorable Mention and the 1988 Golden Poet Award for the poem 'Times Of Wine'. I then won the 1989 Honorable Mention and the 1989 Golden Poet Award for 'The Prayer'. Both of these awards were through The World Of Poetry located Sacremento CA. Both of these poems were published in the then current books being published by The World Of Poetry. In 1997 I entered the poem 'Baren At Sea' in The National Library of Poetry contest. I won the Editor's Choice Award and the poem was published in a book called "Dance Upon the Shore".

In 2004 I entered another contest with The National Library of Poetry and again won the Editor's Choice Award for a poem entitled 'Whispers'. I was included as one of 33 poets whose artistry were recorded professionally as a special part of a new CD poetry collection - "The Sound of Poetry". It was released as a 33-track, three album CD set.

I am very blessed that every time I have thrown a poem out there I have been published. Many people wait very long periods just to be published. One girl who touched my heart the most when it came to poetry was Denise Pollard of Missouri.

She didn't write poetry herself but she hand copied everyone else's poetry into her own journals because of her love of poetry (just to be writing the words of poetry, how humble). I never felt that I loved poetry as much as she did to be able to do such a thing of someone else's writing. I don't think I could deserve to be a writer unless I could love poetry the way she does. I really don't have that kind of love for poetry or qualifications. I just write what comes to me from the heart.